HOPE
after
HURT

FROM HEARTACHE TO HEALING

Roxanne and Rob Maroney

ISBN 978-1-68570-152-9 (paperback)
ISBN 978-1-68570-153-6 (digital)

Christian Faith Publishing
832 Park Avenue
Meadville, PA 16335
www.christianfaithpublishing.com

Printed in the United States of America

For the sake of readability, we use male pronouns when referring to God throughout this book. This is not a sexist statement, nor does it negate any views of our Creator as having all the attributes and character of a nurturing parent, either mother or father.

Roxanne and Rob are the real deal. They offer hope and insight for couples who want to give up. They have something to share because they persevered and faced the pain of growth and took a deep dive into their histories to find the root of their relational struggles. Roxanne and Rob have been close friends for many years, and we have watched the transformation first hand. You will be encouraged and blessed by their story.

MILAN AND KAY YERKOVICH
FOUNDER, RELATIONSHIP 180
AUTHORS OF "HOW WE LOVE" & "HOW WE LOVE OUR KIDS"

We have never been more in need of good stories with great outcomes than we are today. When so many emotional injuries and cultural changes are coupled with so little healthy, long-term modeling, we all flail and flounder trying to make relationships work. Your news feed is full of these ideas that quickly disappoint. However, in *Hope After Hurt: From Heartache to Healing*, you will find Biblical direction, well tested over time, that gradually delivers on its promise. This is not a quick and easy, one and done journey, but no worries, if you don't get it the first time, the lessons will just keep coming, and Roxanne and Rob's story will be there to support you.

DAVE CARDER
MARRIAGE AND FAMILY THERAPIST
AUTHOR OF "TORN ASUNDER, RECOVERING
FROM AN EXTRAMARITAL AFFAIR"

There is an old saying about leadership that, "You can't lead someone where you haven't been". Having known Roxanne and Rob for years, and knowing their marriage journey, they are more than qualified to lead you from a marriage that is good to great, or from bad to better. Their understanding, practical steps, and wisdom will give you tools that can bring vital change to your marriage. The only thing stopping your healthy marriage is a little humility and some good old fashioned wisdom that you'll find in *Hope After Hurt: From Heartache to Healing*.

ERIC HEARD
MARRIAGE PASTOR
MARINERS CHURCH, IRVINE, CA

At last, a book that really is honest about the real stuff couples wrestle with. Thank you, Roxanne and Rob, for having the courage to share the crucible of your journey—educating, equipping, and encouraging us to know that through God's amazing grace, there truly is *Hope After Hurt*.

RANDELL D. TURNER, PH.D.
FOUNDER & CEO
TRANSFORMING FAMILIES

Roxanne and Rob have given the great gift of insight into a story of success in the midst of anguishing marital grief. Why do some marriages make it from sadness to gladness? This book delves into the answer!

WALTER T LINN, PH.D., D.MIN.
MARRIAGE AND FAMILY THERAPIST
FOUNDER & PRESIDENT, GENESIS COUNSELING SERVICE

Are you looking for *hope* that your marriage can get back on track? If your answer is "yes", pick up *Hope After Hurt: From Heartache to Healing*. Roxanne and Rob Maroney candidly unpack the extra baggage they brought into their marriage and share how they navigated difficult obstacles that took their marriage in a new direction. They have a passion to help couples, just like you, experience hope in their once hopeless marriage.

JIM AND DEBBIE HOGAN
CO-FOUNDERS
STANDING STONE MINISTRY

In *Hope After Hurt: From Heartache to Healing*, Roxanne and Rob offer hope to couples struggling in marriage, even if all hope feels lost. Through the vulnerable sharing of their own marriage hardships, and healing recovery process, along with companion stories from the decades of experience helping other couples transform, Roxanne and Rob have written a must read guide for marriage.

QUENTIN HAFNER
MARRIAGE AND FAMILY THERAPIST
AUTHOR OF "BLACK BELT
HUSBAND: A MARRIAGE BOOK FOR MEN"

You are about to journey through anticipation, joy, sadness, hurt, despair, loneliness, connection, relief, and *Hope after Hurt*! This is a must read for any couple whether struggling or not!

DR. DAVID E. RICE, PH.D.
MARRIAGE AND FAMILY THERAPIST
SOUTH COAST PSYCHOLOGICAL CENTER, IRVINE, CA

CONTENTS

ACKNOWLEDGMENTS

God is always, has been, and will be, the greatest and most gracious change agent. To Him be the glory!

No one makes it through life alone, and we are deeply grateful to our family, friends, coworkers, mentors, and advisers who each played an important part in our relational healing. We are also thankful for those who came alongside and supported us in telling our story, encouraging honesty and vulnerability, authenticity and transparency. You all contribute to our lives in profound ways, and you help us never lose sight that there truly is hope after hurt.

To our children, who are patient and forgiving of us as we strive to grow and become better versions of ourselves, thank you. Each of you has traveled different seasons of this journey with us and has experienced us in your own unique ways. We love you and are proud of you.

We are forever grateful to our friend Larry Crabb, who interrupted our lives at just the right time. Through his writing and his wise, loving counsel, he helped us make a shift in our relationship that set us on the course for change. He reminded us of the NewWay. His passing was a great loss, and we miss him, but I've never met anyone who was more ready for heaven.

Thank you to our good friends, neighbors, travel partners, and coworkers Milan and Kay Yerkovich for introducing us to our love styles and helping us learn to break free of old patterns and learn a new dance.

Gratitude to our good friend Paul Danison for applying his thirty years of wisdom and experience as an editor and journalist to help make our story clear, especially when it wasn't. It's good to have smart and competent friends in your life. You've forgotten more about writing than we'll ever know!

To Roxanne's "sacred group" of women who have walked alongside her for fifteen years and to her spiritual director Shaleen for her warm counsel, encouragement, and insightful editing. Thank you.

It's a blessing and privilege to go through life with trusted close friends. Thanks to Rob's group of men who have been in his life regularly for eighteen years, who are a source of continuous encouragement and support. Two thumbs-up to you guys!

Finally, we are grateful to our friend Randy Turner for his encouragement and support to write this book. Your insight, guidance, and belief in us along the way were invaluable.

INTRODUCTION

Roxanne

Brokenness is the awareness that you long to be someone
you're not and cannot be without divine help.

—Larry Crabb, *Shattered Dreams*

More than we know, or at least like to admit, we live in the
shadow of our early histories. Many psychologists theorize
that the first ten years of life are the most important and impressionable when it comes to forming healthy and secure relationships
later in life. Recent research has even shown that the first two to three
months of life create the imprints we carry for a lifetime. These early
years are when the brain is forming neural pathways that equip us to
trust, bond with others, relate with empathy, resolve conflict, manage our emotions, and so much more.

Although I wasn't aware of it then, as I looked back on those
early years of my life, I realized I arrived at some major conclusions
about relationships, trust, shame, fear, and life in general, mostly
from what I witnessed living in a broken family. In my twenties, I
heard marriage would be as easy or difficult as my childhood, so I
concluded marriage was not in the cards for me. I was too flawed, too
jaded to beat the odds. I also recall hearing that because of my parents, I had a greater-than-average chance of becoming an alcoholic
or marrying one, which became another compelling reason to avoid

the whole proposition. Both my parents were married four times, so I had serious doubts about the whole institution of marriage.

Rob, on the other hand, was much more optimistic about marriage. His parents were married sixty-two years until his father died. He came from what he considered a *normal* family, but his definition of *normal* was to be challenged in the years ahead. Although his parents stayed together, the family was emotionally disconnected, leading Rob to accept that marriage might mean living together as compatible roommates, even if unhappy.

Despite my history and apparent obstacles, I fell in love and said *yes* to marriage, hoping my experience would be different, but the seeds of fear remained. Although I've altered and added to my beliefs over the years, the ones I really lived by at my core remained unchanged. I knew I was broken, but I didn't understand exactly where or how to change. Not until after much pain and the desire to grow did I realize I needed to root out some of those false beliefs from my heart and mind one errant strand at a time.

As we talk about our brokenness, what do we mean? It *doesn't* simply mean extreme remorse or sadness, regret or shame, or being at a low place in life. All these emotions were at work in me, and yet I remained stuck. I think of brokenness as the awareness of how my broken environment affected me, as well as acknowledging my humanness, blind spots, and yes, sin, without detouring into shame and self-pity. I came into this world as a precious newborn but determined to have my own way. Gradually and continually, however, I surrendered to a better way. Some of my first lessons of healing involved learning and accepting where I was flawed so I could then move to embrace something higher, something better, something enduring. I came into this broken, tainted, imperfect world like a wild rose, untamed and subject to the environment around me. But the process of healthy brokenness is recognizing my need to submit to the loving hand of a gardener's pruning shears, not to destroy but to be set free to flourish.

This is not just the story of two people who were damaged and in need of repair but two people freed up enough from their pasts to experience healing and restoration. The first two chapters are not meant to be a self-indulgent stroll down memory lane but a way to offer context and hope—hope that change is possible even when the path is littered with potholes and pain. We are the sum total of what we heard, saw, and experienced growing up and the conclusions we came to as a result. But by God's grace, change is possible. I journeyed from victim to victor, although not as quickly as I would have wanted, never arriving at some perfect state but more at peace with the person I'm becoming.

As we share our stories from our individual points of view, some memories will be repeated. We did this because, as with any couple, we experienced these moments together, but we often saw them from different vantage points.

This book is for couples who are in need of a flicker of light in a dark or stuck marriage. Is there hope after hurt? The answer is a resounding *yes*. We hope this account of our journey, the challenges and battles we faced in our marriage, and the choices we made to alter our course will encourage any soul who takes the time to read it. I pray it gives the encouragement that you too can tackle your own internal scars and come out the other side whole and at peace with yourself despite enduring imperfections. After over four decades of marriage, our experiences continue to increase our hope and confidence that love and freedom are possible but not without work and intentional effort. Rob and I entered into a broken world with parents who were broken themselves by their own pasts and histories, and only the grace and love of God could bring greater awareness, increased hope, and the power to change.

Discussion questions

At the end of each chapter, we have included discussion questions. We cover many topics in this book, so as you review each chapter, we encourage you to keep a small notebook of your thoughts and any new awareness. Even if you don't consider yourself a writer, jotting down thoughts, prayers, questions, and discoveries will help you make progress. It has been my experience that when I didn't take time to write down and reflect on what I was learning, I just had to learn those lessons all over again. Journaling helps you slow down, even for a brief period, to breathe, reflect, and listen for the truth. We hope you will give it a try.

A MARRIAGE SHORT STORY

Roxanne

We said, "I do," one bright California morning in 1975. The only available time at the church was 10:00 a.m., and it was a short no-frills event. The reception that followed lasted at most an hour and was not the kind of elaborate event you see at weddings today. No music, dancing, speeches, or toasts—just a few well-wishes from around fifty good friends and family, along with an assortment of nuts, mints, punch, and cake. With hope-filled hearts, we drove off, waving goodbye in our used 1969 Chevy.

We didn't realize it at the time, but we were each towing an invisible trailer full of our stuff from the past. They say love is blind, but we were not only blind to the stuff each other was carrying, we didn't see what we were bringing into this relationship ourselves from our own pasts. We heard all the warnings of the trials and challenges that lie ahead in marriage, but we also believed the Bible says to forget what lies behind and strive to move forward, so ready or not, we drove on.

In time, the road got a little rougher; our *invisible* trailers began to collide. Sometimes there would be a flat tire and some of our stuff would shake loose, but we didn't know where it came from, why it was there, or understood what it meant.

As much as I wanted to show love, joy, peace, patience, kindness—the fruit of the Spirit—something Rob would do or say would cause a miniexplosion inside me, and my response would be irritation, hurt, or withdrawal. I thought at the time my reaction was justified because of what he did, so we played the blame game, comparing whose actions were worse, but inside, I knew something was up with me.

Still towing our invisible trailers, we looked surprisingly good on the outside. Within just a few years, there were three children, we upgraded to the old familiar family minivan, got a mortgage, and drove on living a *normal* middle-class life, all the while leading lives of quiet discontent. I was hoping for more emotional intimacy in the marriage, but Rob struggled to know what true intimacy looked like. We both lived in the shadow of our histories and the cultural messages we came to believe, seasoned by our broken thinking. Those beliefs, scars, and habits were slowly eroding the foundation of our marriage. We wanted our relationship to be different, but it felt like we were fighting an invisible enemy.

> When you don't know what to do you just
> put one foot in front of the other, until one day
> you can't even do that.

The shame and guilt of seeing other happy couples became too much for me, and I eventually just wanted to run far, far away. But I had three children to think of, and I knew in my heart of hearts I had things to face in myself.

In one attempt to get his attention, I wrote this story and gave it to Rob. This was a particularly rough place in our relationship, but I wanted to tell him how I was feeling. This was my way of saying, "I'm sinking, but you seem to not notice."

September 1995

> Picture a beautiful tranquil lake perfect for
> water skiing, with tree-lined shores and dozens
> of coves and inlets just waiting to be discovered.
> Rob and I are out on the lake, he's driving the
> ski boat. I'm doing my best at waterskiing, but
> having trouble getting up and being swamped

with water each time I try. As the water continues pounding my face, it becomes harder to see, and the constant pull of the rope is making it harder and harder to hold on. I wish I could either be good enough to get up on my skis and effortlessly glide behind the boat, or give up altogether and peacefully sink in the water. I could then just relax, the boat could speed away, and I could float in the water without the constant reminder of what a poor skier I am. It's not fun floating alone, but at least it's less stressful.

I finally give in, let go of the rope... I sink and slowly start to float. The noise settles down, it gets quiet in the water, and I wait for him to circle around to come back for me. But as I watch him drive away I realize he hasn't even noticed I've dropped off. Something else seems to be driving him, and he's distracted by other things. Maybe it's something alluring that I'm not seeing, or maybe he's still looking for that sense of significance he never seems to be able to find, or just the thrill and distraction of a fast ride.

This has become a familiar place. Although I think I should wait for him to return, I'd actually rather swim back to the shore and find a place to rest.

The major problem with this recurring situation is that we're pretending...pretending we are a good partnership...pretending we are enjoying each other...pretending we are unified and in love with each other when there is little and infrequent physical contact. Although I know he loves me, the pressure of family life, work, and money makes escaping in a fast boat more attractive. He becomes driven to distract himself from something nagging within that he can't put his finger on.

He occasionally drives by, and we talk about the kids, his job, the weather and sometimes us. But unless I bring it up, we don't discuss the stuff in our relationship that is keeping us apart...the real stuff between us. In the past, I attempted to get back in the boat to be closer to him, but eventually I would get bumped out while he drove off toward something new. I try to hang on to the rope and try to ski again, but it's futile. I'm tired, my strength is fading, and again, I let go and sink into the water.

When the kids were little, it was much easier and enjoyable to all be together. But as the children are in their teen years, we are fortunate to even have a meal together. I see other families in their boats looking like they're having fun and I can't understand why he would rather drive off by himself. But he says he has a lot on his mind and the time alone helps him think. Besides, he says it's easier to drive the boat alone.

Sometimes we join with other boats. We socialize and have a moment of togetherness. But eventually he's off again by himself and I'm back in the water. We both recognize things aren't right, but since it doesn't feel like a real crisis, we don't ask for help from anyone else or share our real feelings with others. But in my desperate moments I look for a lifeguard who can show me what's wrong, or I pick up books on happy family boating, or how to be a better water skier. These efforts sometimes help me for a short while, but ultimately there is little change, and we go back to our familiar ways, like a well-worn path.

I get most concerned when I see other boaters getting older who increasingly follow this same pattern as they age. It seems to become easier and easier as the years go by until eventually they have built separate lives, their paths rarely cross, and at best they become roommates, or split up completely.

Part of me still desperately wants to be close and intimate with him, but to be honest, I'm afraid of being pushed aside again. Although I know his intent is not to reject me, his preoccupation to distract himself still hurts, and my emotional muscles are getting tired.

So, I'm left with the unsatisfying options of getting better at holding on to the rope, faking it, giving up, or building a life for myself in the water, and learning to be content with unsatisfying drive-by conversations. None seem like good choices, and it's a lonely existence.

This cry for help came from my determination to not feel abandoned. Although this picture I painted seemed true, I also had some unhealthy (and untrue) beliefs and conclusions about relationships: conclusions about trust, security, abandonment, and what I could rely on from another person in those relationships. These beliefs and conclusions were now being triggered by Rob's distraction and indifference.

Let's unpack the trailers

Finally reaching the point when I realized I needed help, one bright morning in 1985, I sat in a counselor's office for the first time. He gently helped me look into my trailer. This set me on the course of discovery and freedom. In the beginning, I wanted to believe I could pray it all away or deny it, but I knew I had some work to do to become free from the lies and triggers that haunted me.

These hurts and expectations had taken up residence in my heart long before we ever got married, and they were showing up in real time and playing out in our relationship in an unhealthy dance pattern we repeated over and over for years. I knew I had areas of growth, and I needed to rewrite some false beliefs, but I was also hoping Rob would be the one person who would change all that. I hoped he would be the one who treated me with such unconditional love and care that my insecurities and pain from childhood would finally evaporate. This is a heavy burden to place on another person. I had to unpack my trailer, and Rob had his own trailer of stuff to discover, as you will hear from him.

CHAPTER 1

The Girl in Black and Blue

Roxanne

On that early morning in 1953, as the morning sun came streaming through the window, my exhausted mother who had labored all night finally gave birth to me in a small downtown Los Angeles hospital. Their long-awaited little girl had finally arrived with dark curly hair and chubby cheeks, unaware and unprepared for the troubles ahead. My mother struggled to name me, and nothing seemed to fit until she found the name *Roxanne* in a baby book. Since I was born at sunrise, the meaning caught her eye: "coming with the dawn."

Life was relatively peaceful by this time following the chaos of World War II and everything my parents had endured. They claimed they planned to have a girl to balance out their ideal family of two boys and a girl. They brought me home to a small bungalow-style home in the Los Angeles suburbs. My parents weren't wealthy, and they both worked hard to provide a life neither of them enjoyed when they were young.

My father (Eddie) was an Armenian born in Turkey and forced to flee the country when he was two with his family during the genocide. Coming to the United States, he was raised with a new Americanized name and lived between two cultures. When my parents met many years later, he was much older than my mom (Gloria).

My dad was back home after serving in World War II, and they met over fancy drinks and the music of Benny Goodman at the Cocoanut Grove restaurant in Los Angeles when my mom was just twenty-one.

Gloria and Eddie were forging a life for themselves, and everything seemed to be ideal in the little house in El Sereno, California. I have no conscious memory of that time, although the black-and-white photos portray happy times, backyard parties, and smiling children. All those times ended abruptly the day my mother and I were diagnosed with tuberculosis. No one knows exactly how we contracted the disease, but she was infected and passed it on to me. My brothers and father were spared. As part of her treatment, she was swept away to the City of Hope hospital, not to be seen for a year, and at fifteen months, I was hospitalized and put in isolation for about three months.

In an instant, everything changed

In an instant, all that was known, familiar, or comforting was gone, replaced by sterile walls and masked nurses. I was sick and all alone, confused with no way to understand or put words to my emotions. That was the first of many experiences of helplessness, confusion, and fear I would endure. For years, I minimized this event, thinking all babies are resilient and I survived, but I now understand the importance of the baby years in terms of attachment, security, and brain development even though I have no conscious memory of those months in the hospital.

I cannot imagine how my father coped during this time. He was forty-five when I was born, and now at forty-seven, he had three small children, an ill and absent wife, a business to run, and few skills of comfort or faith from his family of origin for himself or for us. As children, we were left with caregivers, but I was so young, I don't remember many details. My older brothers recall physical care (food, shelter, clothing) at best, but we were feral children in every other respect. After a year of loss and separation, my mother returned home, but it was not to a smiley curly-haired baby. She came home to a shy and angry toddler.

When I was five, we moved again to a larger home in North Hollywood. All the houses in this neighborhood were custom designs on large properties bordered with massive eucalyptus trees lined up like soldiers. The new home was a sprawling ranch with room to spare, a tennis court, pool, and large climbing trees. With the addition of a family pet, a boxer named Duchess, it was a paradise for kids. I had a spacious room all to myself with a large picture window overlooking the backyard pool. On sweltering summer days, we lived in and out of the water like amphibians. On the surface all was idyllic; my parents were moving up the ladder of success as though all their sickness and troubles were behind them, but the rumblings of trouble were beginning again. Just minor tremors at first, but they turned into major seismic events within a few years.

Unknown to all of us, my mother was privately struggling with an anxiety disorder. She later said the pressure of attempting to make up for lost time because of her illness as well as her own demons from childhood caused her periodic panic attacks. One day while experiencing a particularly tough bout, she attended a PTA meeting in another mother's home. Unlike any PTA meeting I ever attended, she was offered a martini, and her fear magically subsided, the clouds parted, the sun was shining—she felt all was well. This was the flash point of the downward spiral. She had discovered a new way to cope with her fear, guilt, and shame, and it was as easy as an occasional sip of clear liquid hidden in orange juice or straight from the bottle when she thought no one was looking.

It all seemed so normal

By the age of five, I was fun loving but cautious. I had a quirky sense of humor and could be entertaining, but if I were too winsome, my two older brothers made sure to put me in my place. Their common nickname for me was *Ug*, which was short for ugly. The only thing I recall my parents saying was, "They only tease you because they love you," which made no sense to me as I fought back tears, wishing they would love me less.

As the youngest of three and the only girl, you would think I would have had some special status, but my brothers had been scarred as well, and left to their own devices, they learned to embrace anger as a friend. I was slight and fairly small for my age with long curly hair often pulled back in a braid to keep it from running wild. But by the time I was six, I developed ninja-type skills at predicting my mother's moods. Was she sober? Was she shaking? Was she irritable? Was she nice? For a while, she didn't drink on Sundays, possibly for some religious reasons, but that day too was soon swallowed up with vodka.

We were a family, sort of. Dad worked extremely hard running his own business, and Mom (when she was sober) was an excellent homemaker, a great cook with an artful eye for decorating. She took great pleasure in dressing me like a doll and taking me shopping. From her description, I was calm and long-suffering, and I became a distraction from the anxiety that followed her like a cloud.

Looking back, I can see I was much more like a therapy dog or a security blanket for her. How ironic, that she placed her security in the child who was in need of security. Losing her for a year when I was a baby had planted seeds of anxiety in my unconscious brain, and I was constantly fearful she would disappear again. If I called for her and couldn't find her in our big sprawling home, my childish mind envisioned that she had dropped through a hole in the floor and was gone forever, probably trace memories of my days in the hospital as an infant.

As our family limped along, still trying to appear normal, I remember fun trips to Disneyland, Las Vegas, and the Grand Canyon. My father also loved the Dodgers, and when I was five, we all attended a Dodgers game at the Coliseum. I was too little to appreciate the sport, but I liked that we were all together, doing something fun where we could eat peanuts and drop the shells on the ground. Then it happened; the announcer introduced the next batter, "Batting for the Dodgers, Jim Gilliam." Moments later, I heard the crack of his bat and saw a ball flying high through the air, quickly descending in our direction.

The moments that followed are a blur: people clamoring, yelling, and reaching for the missile coming our way. All I knew to do was stay low, and as if in slow motion, the ball missed all those reaching arms and crash-landed on my head. I was stunned at first and then began to wail. Although I appeared fine, the stadium authorities insisted I be taken to the nearby hospital to be examined.

As the pain subsided and I calmed down, I must have cooperated with the medical staff because I remember one of the X-ray technicians telling me that he could tell I came from a stable home because I was so calm. In my five-year-old mind, I thought, *Are you kidding? You are so wrong. If you only knew.* For some reason, even though I had no power over the direction of the ball, I felt it was my fault our fun day at the ballpark was cut short.

Now it's not so normal

On most school days, my brothers and I took the bus, leaving my mother to her own madness all day. Often, by the time we came home, it was too dangerous and volatile to be inside with her, so my brothers and I would sit on the curb outside, waiting for my dad to get home. He would scoop us up and take us to dinner at Bob Burns, an upscale diner. Even in a crisis, he preferred fine dining to fast food. Most of the time, however, I was too anxious to eat, much to his displeasure.

The downward spiral

My only real solace and security was our dog Duchess, a boxer with love and energy to spare but fiercely protective of this troubled pack she belonged to. She was the only constant in my life, always there, always loving, always playful. She was so uncomplicated, unlike most of the people around me. If I cried, she cried; if I was happy, she was happy; if a stranger came to the door, watch out. I wonder if she was one of God's gifts for me at that time, loving and protective in a way my human family wasn't. Sadly, one of my strongest attachments was to a dog for most of my childhood, which I'm sure made human relationships much more complicated and difficult. This would rise up to haunt my marriage in the future.

As the fear and mental illness of addiction increased its stranglehold, my mother became more and more desperate. Late one night in one of her manic states when I was six years old, she grabbed me out of bed with car keys in hand. No explanation was offered, just a hurried desperation in her voice. Confused and frightened, I complied, too young and too scared to object. We drove through the dark, empty streets of Los Angeles to a large Catholic church.

I had never been inside a church before, let alone one so dark and cavernous. Why was it open in the middle of the night? No one was inside, and there was only the flicker of candlelight to guide us as we slowly walked down the aisle. When we reached the front, I slipped into a pew by myself as she continued all the way up to the front. I didn't understand why we were there or what she was doing, but most of all, I was confused by the larger-than-life-sized statue of a man hanging on the wall with blood dripping down his face.

The whole scene was surreal. I was so young. I was so frightened. There was nothing calming or comforting in this strange environment. As I sat low in my seat trying to wish myself away, my mother suddenly let out a scream of desperation, pleading with God to help her. I was undone. I could not run. I could not cry out myself, and I was trapped in this awful nightmare with nowhere to go, nowhere to hide. My childlike brain couldn't make sense of this strange scene, and my understanding of God at this point didn't offer any comfort, only confusion.

> Parents are supposed to be a source of comfort and support. My mom was a strange mixture of love and terror. I needed a mom to survive, but mine was preoccupied with her own personal hell. One thing I knew for sure, she could not be trusted, and I dreamed of being in a safe place somewhere else.

The chaos builds

Life at this point was dangerous, unpredictable, but most of all, confusing. I'm sharing this part of the story because it shows God's love and pursuit in the midst of pain and how amazing it is that I ever became open to spiritual matters. I also share this to emphasize how the things we see, hear, and experience in our family growing up create an imprint on our hearts, impacting how we seek connection and build relationships.

A chain is only as strong as its weakest link, making my family chain very fragile. Being older than the average dad, my father had already experienced the atrocities of World War II in active duty in the Pacific. Wanting to put the ugliness of war behind him, he never spoke about what he saw, but the few stories I heard from other family members were enough pain and loss for a lifetime. Now he was embroiled in a different kind of war, but he was losing this battle.

Dad never knew what awaited him when he came home from work. The chaos of our lives was fraying and tearing apart the fabric of his soul. Although not a violent man, his anger ignited when Mom put me in harm's way or neglected me when I was sick. Her drunken tirades often triggered violent exchanges between them. I have a clear mental image of a slapping match on the front lawn between my mom and dad trading blows as if in some sick game, driven by their anger and passion, and no thought of the family or neighbors who were watching. Wearing only slacks and a white bra, eventually stained bright-red from her bloody nose, my mother kept fighting until a neighbor called the police, and she was taken away in handcuffs. The strange thing is I can't remember what happened next. No conversation, no explanation, no one asking if we were okay—everyone just drifted off to cope with the experience alone. It was fright with no antidote, no comfort, no solution.

Mother would frequently be gone for a few days to dry out only to return with promises of being "all better" but with a simmering anger over feeling betrayed. She never remembered the pain she inflicted on others, only what was done to her. I'm sure her memory of those events was fragmented because of the alcohol, but these images and experiences were seared into my brain like a video cued to play if you hit just the right button.

When I was six, I had a girlfriend named Lisa, who lived a few miles away. I played at her house occasionally, and one day, we were having a wonderful time when my mother showed up and said I needed to go with her. She was incoherent, and Lisa's mom became worried about my safety and secretly called my dad to ask him what to do. He asked her to call the police because he worked too far away to be of any immediate help. The scene that unfolded was ugly. Several police arrived, and Mom became like a provoked caged tiger, growling and struggling, barking out in slurred speech, and I was caught in the middle of this struggle on Lisa's front lawn for all her neighbors to see. I was amazed at how an average-size woman with enough alcohol can fight off four uniformed police officers.

After an intense struggle, she eventually lost her stranglehold on my arm and was taken away in handcuffs. Lisa's mom, fully unprepared for this scene, did her best to calm me. She made cookies, and we went for a walk until my father could pick me up. As we walked around the block, her neighbors peeked out their windows to watch the remaining characters of this sad drama. This was one of many times I wished for a magic cloak to throw around myself to become invisible. So much shame and embarrassment.

This became another experience recorded in my memory, serving as a reminder that my family was different from others. Looking back, I appreciate Lisa's mom and her concern for my safety. Sadly, however, I was never asked to play with Lisa again.

Alliances and protest

"The boys"—meaning, my dad and brothers—had their own alliance in this storm, and they found ways to get away from the ugliness of our chaotic home, usually involving sports. I felt like the fifth wheel, which left me the odd "little girl" out, fending for myself when her drinking would escalate. At six years old, I already suffered from migraine headaches, stomachaches, anxiety, and sleeplessness. Other than what I had seen in movies, I didn't understand much about war, but I felt like I was fighting in one, and I had about as much chance of winning as fighting a forest fire with a squirt gun.

My brothers, on the other hand, were old enough to resist Mom's aggression, especially when they banded together against her. My oldest brother, Danny, came to my aid a few times to prevent me from being hurt, but compared to what happened when they weren't home, those moments of rescue were infrequent. I tried to protest and run away at times, but that turned out to be a big mistake. As soon as I was alone with her, she would lash out with physical abuse and would accuse me of siding with her enemy, my father.

When Mom was drunk, she often squirreled me away in a hall closet, not as punishment but more for safekeeping, like her many bottles of vodka hidden around the house. I was too fearful to leave the closet, knowing I would incur her wrath, so I would sit in the dark until my father came home from work to release me. I see now how my brothers, my dad, and I adapted to chaos in our own ways. Some got angry, some fought back, some ran away or hid, and some, like my mother, got drunk. I didn't realize how these patterns of anger, fighting back, or running away would come back to haunt me over and over again years later in my adult life, especially in my marriage.

The most confusing thing about living with an alcoholic, or any addict, and the chaos it brings is that one day can be almost normal (if there is such a thing) and the next day or moment can be hell on earth. With no way to predict what you will face from day to day, there's no way to prepare. I believe this was the beginning of my sense of shame because as a young girl left alone most of the time, I had limited survival skills. I always felt I was different, that my family was flawed, and I was powerless to change it. I was in a tug of war, and no matter how hard I pulled, I was outnumbered and eventually ended up in the mud puddle. It's one thing to be responsible for my own wrongdoings and suffer the guilt and consequences, but it's another to pay the physical and emotional price for my mother's behavior.

The daily and nightly struggles continued, hindering my ability to think or concentrate in school. I don't recall anyone noticing I was sinking. I imagine I just appeared remedial or suffering from a learning disability. I struggled with spelling in school, which became another mark on my already-bruised self-image. World War III was raging at home, and studying a list of spelling words was not a high priority, so I often failed spelling quizzes. To my amazement, and the teacher's, I finally passed a spelling test one day. The teacher *thoughtfully* announced it to the class by comparing me to another student who also passed, despite the fact the other student hadn't learned to speak English yet. I don't think I could have felt smaller. Shame was like a heavy wet blanket, beckoning me to become more invisible, but at the same time, I was longing just to be seen as normal.

By the time I was seven, the troubling times far outnumbered the good. It was like a symphony orchestra playing out of tune, growing louder and more chaotic, with fewer and fewer moments of pleasant melody, and all the notes were soon clashing. Although there were occasional days of sobriety, especially after being sent away to a hospital to dry out, Mom quickly slid back down the rabbit hole of drinking when she came home. The only time I saw my father cry was when he arrived home from work to find me extremely sick in bed with a high fever, and Mom was too drunk to care for me. His crying unsettled me as he pleaded with her to wake up and care for her kids, like making one last attempt to beg for our lives back. We were all reaching our breaking point.

My dad wasn't prone to violence or drinking, but as her addiction drove him deeper into despair, he lashed out physically more frequently. I remember him throwing her across the kitchen floor and seeing her bounce off the refrigerator. As she lay there in a drunken heap, I remember screaming and choking on my food as the scene played out in slow motion.

Divorce

I don't know when I first learned about divorce, but I remember thinking it must be the only answer. I knew our family couldn't go on this way much longer. The strain on all of us was growing heavier by the day. The arguments between my parents continued, but no one ever talked about it afterward. We just went from one episode to the next with no conversation, no attempt to help us understand, no comfort, just coping at the moment by disappearing into TV or escaping by riding my bike to a friend's house.

The last fibers of the family fabric finally snapped, and my father filed for divorce when I was seven and a half. On the day of the final court hearing, Mom was drunk and didn't even attend, so my father was awarded everything, including custody of all three children. The judge ruled she was an unfit mother and awarded her a small cash settlement and one of the cars.

I don't recall the day Mom left, but she drove away without a goodbye. I don't even recall feeling sad about it. I had lost my mom, but in truth I lost her years before. At least now, what was left of our family could breathe. It would be lonely, but we could breathe.

Forging a new life

Thus, we started our new life: a working single dad and house-keepers for caregivers. They really weren't *caregivers* because other than food and clean clothes, there wasn't much *caregiving* going on. Money wasn't an issue for us, but we were reduced to living a very basic lifestyle, mostly out of convenience. My long curly hair was cut short because my dad didn't know what to do with it, and I felt like the one unique positive quality I had was taken away. I also felt different from my friends at school and other neighborhood kids because none of them had divorced parents. With so many unhappy memories in that home, my dad eventually sold the house, and we moved.

> At times, a change of scenery can help, but when you don't deal with the root of the underlying trauma, it follows you wherever you go. The memories don't go away easily, if ever.

I don't remember much interaction with my brothers during those years. We lived parallel lives, but it seemed my dad found their company more enjoyable than mine. I felt less important because I wasn't a boy; I didn't play baseball or look beautiful like the women in my dad's magazines. To my father's credit, he worked hard, providing a comfortable home, building a successful business, and raising three children as a single parent. He found time for himself through Dodger baseball, Friday night poker games, Frank Sinatra music, and fine food. I don't recall celebrating birthdays or other occasions, but we never worried about our next meal or a roof over our heads. His best attempt at Christmas was a four-foot silver aluminum foil tree with blue balls and a color wheel behind it.

The hills are alive...

In his attempt to create something *normal* after the chaos of those difficult years, my father signed me up in Girl Scouts to provide some "girl things" to do. One spring day, our troop set off for a field trip to see a new movie about a musical family in Austria. All dressed in green, we boarded a bus for a short ride to Hollywood. I loved music; it was one of the ways I coped, listening to albums on a giant hi-fi and imagining a better place, but I had no idea this movie would reveal to me all the longings I had secretly stored up inside.

With popcorn in hand, the movie began as Julie twirled around on top of the mountain and began to sing. I was captured, heart, mind, and soul. This was it; this is what I longed for, to live in a beautiful place, to be part of a singing family, with lots of siblings and a loving caregiver who liked to have fun and was beautiful too. Although this family had also lost their mother, their new nanny took a special interest in the children and cared deeply for each one of them and eventually won the heart of their gruff and stern father. They were living through troubling times to be sure, but they banded together and remained a family as they climbed the Alps to freedom from the enemies who wished to tear them apart.

I couldn't have written a more perfect antithesis to my own story. This wasn't a fairy tale like Cinderella; this was a true story about real people who had real problems. This family was broken by their mother's death, but unlike mine, this story had a loving ending. Somehow, *The Sound of Music* became the catalyst for my decision to major in music in high school and college. I had musical ability. I could carry a tune, stay in pitch, and had a natural rhythm. Somehow, if only for two and a half hours, I was transported into beauty and belonging. I longed to replicate that feeling in real life because my reality was quite different, and I continued trying to find peace and belonging in any way I could.

Frankie

Attempting to heal from all we had gone through, my father reached out to Al-Anon, a support group for spouses married to alcoholics. He met a woman there named Frankie, who had also suffered the pain of alcoholism in her previous marriage. Both of them were looking for healing from their previous failed marriages, and this group helped them process their pain together. They forged a meaningful friendship, later leading to romance and marriage.

I am still mystified by what my father did or said to convince Frankie to marry him and take on a new family with our issues, but when I was about twelve and my brothers were sixteen and seventeen, she agreed to marry him. We had lived without a mother or any female influences for about five years, and other than the fear of making Dad mad, we had very few limitations or family rules. We were a family in the loosest sense of the word.

I genuinely liked her and I think she liked me, although I was careful not to demand much for fear of rejection. The feeling of being a normal family returned, with dinners together and all. We celebrated holidays and birthdays, and I had some stylish clothes for the first time in my life. I credit some of my sanity to her.

Off to Europe

Although the world was in chaos during this time due to the war in Vietnam, civil rights issues, and protests for peace, these were stable years for me. Junior high school seemed to fly by, not like the snail's pace of grammar school, and by the time I graduated the *tween* years and started high school, my teeth were straight, braces were off, my awkward frame had been replaced with curves, and I found my voice in many ways. My days were a mixture of social events, music performances, and hanging out at Malibu or Zuma Beach. I found ways to calm my fears from the past by distracting myself with busyness and activities with friends. But my lingering insecurities weren't far beneath the surface.

My experience with my mom and her relationship with alcohol made me cautious about drinking and wild parties. I was determined not to become like her. I also avoided crossing the line sexually, afraid of getting pregnant. Fear was a familiar motivator for me, and God was not even part of my thinking at that time. My grandmother made repeated attempts to influence us spiritually and would call whenever Billy Graham was on TV, but we politely ignored her invitations to watch. Maybe we all were too resentful for everything that happened, or we just didn't care, but either way, I had no desire or interest in exploring the spiritual part of my life. I was getting along just fine, or so I thought.

On a blistering hot day in June 1970, I graduated with honors from North Hollywood High School, partly due to hard work but also the desire to prove myself. High school was a rite of passage, and I didn't appreciate how hard it would be to leave that cozy environment and enter the big unknown. I had no idea what I wanted to do, and I underestimated the fear of going it alone as all my friends were scattering to the four winds.

I applied for college and was accepted to several, but my father objected to women attending college. In his old-country way of thinking, he wasn't convinced it was a good return on investment. If I was going to college I had to do it on my own. Once again, I was faced with loss and being left on my own.

In my last year of high school, I was offered the opportunity to travel to Europe with a singing group, so after graduation, I set off for a six-week tour of Europe. I decided to make a decision about college when I returned. Given the right circumstances, even the most gaping holes in a soul can be masked with enough distractions. The six weeks of touring in Europe and performing were enlightening, fun, and filled with constant activities. The first night in Vienna standing alone on the cobblestone street just outside our hotel, I felt like Dorothy in the Land of Oz. I looked up at the moon in the midnight sky and couldn't believe it looked the same when my surroundings were so completely different. I was exhilarated like a bird out of a cage for the first time. My wings felt like they were beginning to flap a bit, seeing parts of the world I never thought I would.

Upon returning home from Europe with all the fun and adventure in the rearview mirror, the road ahead was unknown and unclear. The boy I was dating was convinced we would marry one day. He did not know I had made a vow to stay single since I had such a jaded view of relationships from what I'd seen in my family. Although we were never officially engaged, I humored his vision, especially since he had been drafted into the army and was soon leaving for basic training and then to Vietnam. I cared for him and worried about his future, but I knew we were too young and confused to even consider any long-term relationship.

Panic!

The night he left, a group of us had dinner together, said goodbye, and I headed home. I felt a bit sad but for the most part, unaffected. Around 2:00 a.m., I woke up in a full-blown panic attack. I don't know if it was connected to his departure or the uncertainty of the future, but it seemed to come out of the blue. I now understand that the past is not the past if it invades the present. These circumstances created a perfect storm where my experiences of abandonment, loss, shame, and rejection erupted like an angry volcano, and the distractions that used to mask my insecurities were ripped away.

That night as I struggled to breathe and make sense of what was happening, I felt like I was drifting in the middle of the Pacific, no land in sight and nothing but a small raft with no oars. I had no solid plans, little parental support, no idea what I wanted to do or be, and no one to give me direction. Now one of my close friends was leaving for an unknown, uncertain, and dangerous mission.

> Here I was again, struggling with the fears I held inside about being left, being without support or guidance, and it was all rushing to the surface. This was another reminder of the haunting belief: people leave; people leave me; people leave me and don't return. These fears ignited a firestorm of anxiety.

For the next six months, I limped along, working a meaning-less job in a department store, selling towels. My underlying anxiety came and went but never went away entirely. I often struggled to keep food down or to have an appetite at all. I had become painfully thin. Counseling for mental or emotional issues didn't seem to be as readily available at the time, and I thought it was reserved for really desperate and extreme cases, so I didn't share how bad I really felt for fear of judgment.

Was I following in my mother's footsteps? Was I crazy? I wanted to just snap out of it but I didn't know how. I was certain I wasn't going to take my mother's way of escape because I knew where it led, so I got really good at faking it. I became an actress in a perfor-mance. I smiled on the outside but was plagued with self-doubt on the inside.

There are three common questions that contribute to forming an unhealthy self-image: Am I unlovable? Am I helpless? Am I unwor-thy? Not everyone struggles the same way with all these, but looking back, I see how I wrestled with all three. Based on what I heard, saw, and experienced growing up, I had embraced some unhealthy and inaccurate beliefs about my value, my capability, and my worth. I could either launch a campaign to disprove all these or give in and become a victim of the false beliefs. Out of sheer determination, I learned to push through my fears and gut it out, but that alone wasn't changing my lack of confidence and insecurity.

The tour guide needs a guide

After the Europe tour, I started attending college near my home, still working at that same boring job in a department store. The memories of traveling and playing music in Europe all seemed to fade, and I was now just marking time. A friend from college told me about a job as a tour guide at Universal Studios that paid well, so she encouraged me to apply. Despite my self-doubt, I applied for the job, mostly to pay for college and get out of what I thought was the most boring job on the planet. I was surprised at my interest in applying for a highly visible position as a tour guide, but deep down inside, performing came naturally.

As I learned to hide my fear and anxiety, I had honed my skills of faking it, and mixed with years of singing throughout high school, I felt ready to face the fear of public speaking. The best part was if this job worked out, I could leave the confines of my windowless, minimum wage, perpetual towel-folding job in exchange for more money and maybe a bit more fun.

Although this new job wasn't my passion and didn't offer any future direction, it was a step up from what I was doing. For the next four years, I struggled my way through college, still not knowing who I really was or what I wanted to do. Performing weekly, I led tour groups on a large orange Universal Studios tram, making people laugh, distracting them from their lives as we toured the make-believe world of movies.

During these college years, I felt like I was in a waiting room. I wasn't as tortured with anxiety as before, but I still didn't see a path forward; I was waiting for something (or someone) to light the way. I maintained loose connections with friends from work, family, and school, putting one foot in front of the next. I bounced around between being an art major, then music, and then humanities. My father said I was wasting time because "women didn't need to go to college." His lack of support for further education stirred up some doubt in me about my choices but also strengthened my determination to prove him wrong.

Searching for meaning

From the time my mother left when I was eight until eighteen, she tried to build a relationship with me but more as a good friend than a mother. I spent time with her on the weekends but still had difficulty trusting her. She had been sober for a few years, but she was still not a source of emotional support or stability. She was preoccupied with money problems, working to support herself and struggling in her third of four marriages. I optimistically wanted to believe the worst years with her were behind me, but after eight years of sobriety, she relapsed back into her addiction. I caught her sneaking vodka, lying about unimportant things, being overly dramatic, and generally acting the way she did when I was a child.

> I remember thinking I shouldn't be surprised by an alcoholic's behavior, but it still hurt nonetheless and threw me back to my early trauma and triggered some of the same emotions.

Knowing I couldn't stay with her, I packed up the few things I had at her apartment and went back to my dad's house. I felt ashamed over being fooled by her again and needing to ask for my father's help. I was so embarrassed to be returning home; in fact, I knocked on the door as if I didn't belong there or afraid I would hear, "I told you so."

I knew it wasn't my fault she didn't stay sober but it was another reminder of the cracks in my family's foundation and fueled my doubts about whether people really change. I started to question, could I change? It's surprising how one seemingly small thing triggers a tidal wave of emotions, but I was becoming more and more cynical and slightly depressed.

My stepmother felt like a source of stability during this time, and I believed she truly cared for me. Seeing my struggles, she invited me to go to church with her. She attended a small Methodist church she found inspiring, and she hoped I would too. We slipped into the dark wooden pew just as the pastor stepped up to offer his moving message about love.

At this point, I didn't see God's love or care for me. I wasn't thinking much about spiritual things then, but I believed in God and would sometimes pray, but in that moment, something snapped in me, and I concluded there was no God; life was just a random series of events, and I was on my own. The realization I was crossing off the last shred of any hope or belief in a higher power brought me to tears.

I'm sure my stepmother and those around me thought I was moved by the message, but just the opposite was true. When the pastor finally finished, I tried to quickly exit, but an acquaintance from school I didn't know very well approached me and asked what my tears were about. I said I wasn't sure, trying to politely end the conversation. If she hadn't been so compassionate and soft-spoken, I may not have continued the conversation. She extended an invitation to a Bible study the college kids were having on Tuesday night. "No pressure," she added. "If you don't like it, you can leave, no questions asked."

Having denied God's existence just moments before, I don't know why I agreed to go. Maybe the weight of my cynicism was too much or the deep desire for love—or maybe it was God's reaching down to a troubled soul, inviting her out of her personal hell and into a relationship with Him? I now believe it was all three.

Tuesday night arrived, and I reluctantly got in my VW Bug and drove over to the church. I didn't know anyone there except Carol, who had invited me, and it took everything in me to walk into that gathering. I kept asking myself, "Why am I here?" I thought, *This is stupid. I should leave.*

Before I could change my mind, a young man named Mark greeted everyone warmly and asked us to sit down in a circle of pillows on the floor. I thought, *Okay, this is different*, but I still positioned myself near the exit if it got weird or someone put me on the spot. There were about fifteen of us there from various colleges. Everyone looked seemingly *normal*, so I was hoping to blend in or be a fly on the wall.

Mark began teaching from the Bible (I only knew Psalm 23 and the Ten Commandments from my Sunday school days). I can't recall exactly what his talk was about, but I remember thinking it was different than what I'd heard in church; it was more personal, more filled with hope. Toward the end, he asked us to close our eyes as he led us in prayer, inviting us to begin a relationship with God through accepting Christ into our lives. I was so thankful everyone had their eyes closed because I began to cry uncontrollably, trying to hold it back the best I could. I didn't know why I was crying, but it felt like someone was offering me a lifeline.

My faith and trust had been badly damaged by important people in my life who broke promises, but that night at the Bible study,

I fearfully and silently opened my heart to Christ, and thankfully, God accepted my meager offering of faith. For the next month or so, I must have prayed that prayer daily because I was waiting for some miracle, a vision, anything remarkable. I wanted a tangible sign. Instead, I sensed a gradual shift in my desires, and verses from the Bible slowly penetrated my heart. I found I was becoming less cynical and less fearful. Microscopic movements to be sure but clearly different than I'd seen before, and it wasn't coming from me.

A new direction

In the months that followed, I continued my college career as a music major. I was determined to prove to my father I could accomplish something and hoped my love for music and performance would lead to something else. I just didn't know what. I was involved with a Christian organization on campus and learned they had a division dedicated to music. I was excited to hear I could join their staff and use my musical skills in a creative and purposeful way, but I would have to raise my own financial support, and it seemed like such a long shot. I was attracted to the thought of combining both music and my newfound faith, but I knew my father wouldn't understand or approve. I felt I was really stepping out on a limb, but I figured I didn't have anything to lose; he didn't approve of me going to college in the first place.

A leap of faith

Stepping out in faith, I submitted my application. I was accepted and invited to their staff training conference. The cost was minimal, only three hundred dollars for the month-long training, but it seemed like a small mountain to me. I had to take a leave of absence from school in case I changed my mind and break the news to the family.

As expected, they all thought I had lost my mind or had been swept into some crazy cult. But two people were supportive; a friend from work gave me one hundred dollars as a birthday gift, and my grandmother gave me the remaining two hundred dollars. I took this as confirmation of my decision, and with a leap of faith, I drove off for this new adventure.

I still had moments of uncertainty, but something was beckoning me to pursue a life more focused on helping others than living for my own security and status. Little did I realize the importance of this decision or how it would alter the course of my life, who I would meet, fall in love with, and eventually marry.

Six months later, having completed the training and raising my financial support, I attended their annual staff conference in Colorado. This organization is one of the largest in the world, with opportunities for service worldwide. It can be somewhat like joining the military and not knowing where you will be stationed. I had options of music groups in various parts of the US, Europe, and Asia. I didn't find out which one I might be working with until I was invited to a luncheon to meet other members of the group.

I remember the day clearly. There were about fifteen of us sitting around a large U-shaped table, all strangers to each other. The new director announced we would be forming a new group based in Columbus, Ohio, to perform in churches and college campuses throughout the Midwest. I had never ventured out of California very much, and other than a brief trip to Chicago when I was eight, I had never been to this part of the country.

As the group made introductions, one guy stood out to me in a curious way. He was not particularly chatty. I found out later he was struggling with this assignment because he thought he was going overseas to do something entirely different. Have you ever had the experience of meeting a stranger that stands out to you as someone you may know for a long while? It's happened to me only a handful of times, but when it becomes a reality, it sticks in your mind. I didn't really notice anyone else at that lunch, but in my mind, I saw a giant question mark over his head, and I also had a weird hunch I would know him for a very long time. We all left Colorado to return home and get ready to meet up again in six months for more training in California.

Beginning of a new journey

Fast-forward a few months, I arrived at our training center in California, driving up in my tiny yellow Subaru, and that same guy was coming out the front door of the apartment building where we would be living. At first, I thought I was mistaken because he seemed very friendly, not at all like the person at the meet and greet in Colorado. He said his name was Rob, and he had just arrived, flying in from his home state of Indiana. That first evening, a few of us who arrived early had dinner together, and I was pleasantly surprised he didn't seem as weird as I first thought but had a great sense of humor and was really nice.

During those few months of training and rehearsals, I got to know many people in the group, but I still had a singular focus on the job at hand. Since there were so many of us, mostly single, I thought little of Rob's invitation to catch a movie together. I figured he was just making the rounds of meeting all the single girls. Although we had a wonderful time together, my mind was on a different wavelength. Remember, I was not looking for any type of relationship, and marriage was certainly not on my radar screen.

The relationship begins

The group finished our training in California and planned to reconvene again at our assignment in Columbus, Ohio, after the Christmas break. Everyone flew home, and I drove my little Subaru back to Los Angeles to spend the holidays with my family. On Christmas Day, I received a surprise phone call from Rob. I wasn't sure what this special gesture meant, if anything. I thought I was just one of the gang. "Maybe we were just going to be good friends," I said to myself with a shrug.

I had no idea Rob was becoming more serious about our relationship. I was still looking at marriage through the lens of what I saw growing up and the damaged relationship of my mom and dad. My plan was to enjoy this next season but not get entangled with a guy. But his persistent kindness, humor, steadiness, and shared Christian values were slowly winning me over.

We dated for a year as we toured together with our Christian music group. I got to know him in "real life," not just in romantic settings. We saw each other in the good, bad, and ugly. I didn't have any doubts about him as a potential mate, but the fear of marriage still haunted me.

On Valentine's Day he asked me to marry him. I accepted, hoping for the best, but hidden beneath the surface, I feared the worst. I wrestled with trusting God for the first few weeks of our engagement. Eventually, however, I sensed God was bringing us together, and I needed to trust Him with my fears. Rob's history was completely different from mine, but he too had his own form of brokenness, deeply hidden and just as painful.

Discussion Questions

Chapter 1: The Girl in Black and Blue

For personal reflection

1. Are there parts of Roxanne's history you identify with? Which ones?
2. Can you remember a time in your history when your parents gave you comfort for an emotional upset, not just a physical injury? If not, what did you do when you were upset?
3. Parents or others in our families often create more stress than relieve stress. Who in your family caused pain or crisis without helping you process your emotions?
4. How is my current relationship similar or different from my childhood home growing up?

For group discussion

1. What example or model of a healthy relationship did your parents (or someone else) give you? Remember, the absence of all conflict is not entirely helpful either.
2. What were your conclusions about relationships that came from watching your parents?
3. How do you think Roxanne's history set her up for having problems later in her marriage?

CHAPTER 2

Hiding from Shame

Rob

Roxanne and I have worked with hundreds of couples over the years, and as we explore their stories, we ask questions about their childhood, what it was like growing up, and memories of their family and caregivers. We find both men and women often dig in their heels, saying, "the past is the past," or "sure, there were some hard things, but I'm over that now." But we know from their stories that the past is not the past when parts of it still show up in their lives today.

Don't misunderstand us here; we don't believe we are prisoners to our past, but we do believe this: what we saw, heard, and experienced growing up made a deep imprint on us, and it leaks out in the present and in our current relationships.

Roxanne is the mirror to my soul. In addition to being my life partner, intimate companion, and best friend, she has the incredible gift of seeing beneath what most people only see on the surface. She sees places in my heart I work hard to keep hidden from others and buried deep within. She knows me, and I am humbled at how she has faithfully stood by me when I wandered, when I pursued elusive goals, when I was distracted by nonrelational forms of intimacy, when I floundered, and when I finally crashed. My attempt to describe what she means to me always falls short and feels inadequate. I will be forever grateful for her tenderness, her compassion, her insight, her wisdom, her faithfulness, and her love. She has seen my dark side and stayed by me.

While I am incredibly grateful to Roxanne for her patience and forgiveness, she will tell you how she carried her own pain and wounds from her story into our marriage. Neither of us did it perfectly, and sometimes not well at all, but we chose to own our own stuff and face the chaos we had created together. Psychologist and author Dan Allender describes the importance of engaging with our stories:

> Choosing to engage our stories honestly requires a great deal of courage. Choosing a richer life requires revisiting the past, which may reopen painful wounds of failure and betrayal. The only reason worth entering the pain is the hope that somehow it can be transformed, that through it we will learn to love better and will know more joy.[1]

Reading Allender's comments, I became more aware of where my reluctance to share my story came from. I was afraid of revealing something I'm embarrassed to admit. I was afraid if I was honest and vulnerable about my life, I'd be exposed. I was afraid of showing weakness. I was afraid of reliving painful memories and experiencing the pain I might recall. I resisted owning up to where I fell short, where I didn't measure up, where I didn't feel good enough, and where I had hurt the people I loved most. But I resisted exposing my shame. That's it; I resisted the feeling of shame.

Like many other men, in addition to many other things contributing to the struggles in our marriage, my story also includes buried sexual struggles and unresolved pain. I would not have as much to contribute to this book without my own story of sexual brokenness

---

[1]   Dan Allender, *To Be Told* (Waterbrook, 2006).

and recovery. Author and therapist Jay Stringer writes, "Unwanted sexual behaviors are due to the unexamined and therefore unresolved issues in our lives."[2]

My struggle with the pain of unexamined and unresolved issues allowed shame to become one of the most effective weapons to shut me down and cause me to hide. Shame is a profound feeling that I am inherently weak, that I am damaged and unworthy of love. One of the first symptoms of underlying shame is isolation. Shame steals, kills, and destroys our integrity and joy as a man or woman.

In my reluctance to relive and reveal parts of my story, I resisted looking at those things in my heart I didn't want to remember. There are parts I would rather dismiss, gloss over, or even rewrite in my story. But quickly driving past these scenes, as if they didn't exist or had no impact, was not honest and built a wall against the transformational work of God in my life. I believe now more than ever that the past is not the past when it invades the present. It's our prayer that something in our story of rupture, repair, and redemption will give you the courage to press on.

To be seen…to be vulnerable

Roxanne started writing the story of how she processed her experiences growing up in a ruptured family nearly ten years ago. While I supported and encouraged her efforts, I never really recognized how our early histories would become so intricately intertwined and how our stories would merge. Sharing life stories is hard work and *heart* work. Telling the truth is vulnerable. Exposing what's in my heart and letting others see behind the masks I wear is scary.

In his book *The Wounded Heart*, Allender writes, "The work of restoration cannot begin until a problem is fully faced."[3] I'm a fairly guarded person and don't typically rush into the kind of self-disclosure that risks exposing what's going on inside, but this is my quest

---

2   Jay Stringer, *Unwanted* (NavPress, 2018).
3   Dan Allender, *The Wounded Heart* (NavPress, 2018).

to be honest, facing how my past invaded the present and the impact it had on me and our marriage.

Words like *vulnerable* and *authentic* sound easy to use, but what do they really mean? The dictionary defines vulnerability as "the quality or state of being exposed to the possibility of being attacked or harmed, either physically or emotionally." That's an unsettling definition, yet it accurately describes my fear and why I was reluctant and guarded about being vulnerable with my story. Why would I willingly open myself up to being exposed and the possibility of being hurt, attacked physically or emotionally? I'm drawn to the strong sound of virtues like vulnerability and integrity, but I was confused over what these virtues looked like, and I didn't have any role models growing up to show the way.

In my confusion about virtues and to protect myself from being hurt, I locked my heart in a coffin, much the way C. S. Lewis described in *The Four Loves*:

> To love at all is to be vulnerable. Love anything, and your heart will certainly be wrung and possibly broken. If you want to make sure of keeping it intact, you must give your heart to no one, not even to an animal. Wrap it carefully round with hobbies and little luxuries; avoid all entanglements; lock it up in the casket or coffin or your selfishness. But in that casket—safe, dark, motionless, airless—it will change. It will not be broken; it will become unbreakable, impenetrable, irredeemable.[4]

Lewis's quote hits me between the eyes. Love involves risk, but the risk of not loving means your heart changes; it becomes *unbreakable*, but *brokenness* is the pathway to healing. For over a decade, Brené Brown has studied authenticity, and she offers an excellent

---

[4]   C. S. Lewis, *The Four Loves* (Lewis Pte Ltd., 1960).

definition in her book *The Gifts of Imperfection*. Expanding on what it means to be "authentic...your true self," she writes, "Authenticity is the daily practice of letting go of who we think we are supposed to be and embracing who we actually are." Brown goes on to say, "Choosing authenticity means cultivating the ability to be imperfect, allowing ourselves to be vulnerable, and setting appropriate boundaries."[5]

These were all hugely underdeveloped qualities in my life. I resisted imperfection, I wrestled with vulnerability, and I didn't understand boundaries. The more I realized what I didn't understand about authenticity and vulnerability, the more curious I became about how to strengthen these virtues. I saw the damage in my relationships caused by my inability to reveal my authentic self, which eventually reared its ugly head in our marriage many years later in destructive ways.

We have to go back to go forward

A good place for anyone to begin understanding the story of their life is to look at those who came before. I am the firstborn great-grandson of Irish immigrants. My great-grandfather was the first in my family to come to the US from Ireland, and he died at age thirty-six, when my grandfather was only four years old. My grandfather died before I was born, so both my dad and I never knew our paternal grandfathers. It's interesting to see how these little pieces of the puzzle create a bigger picture when you start putting them together. With these weak missing links in my family history, both my dad and I shared a weak sense of heritage, a weak appreciation for family history, and had little value for family tradition.

---

5 Brené Brown, *The Gifts of Imperfection* (Hazelden, 2010).

I grew up as the middle child with two sisters. Both parents were in the home, but my dad was emotionally disconnected and had abdicated his responsibility to be a source of emotional support. My mom wasn't a particularly forceful or assertive woman, but between her and my older sister, there was a definite female dominance in the home. Both of my grandmothers were strong, independent, assertive women, whose husbands were both passive and detached, and both died at an early age.

I was an overweight kid and didn't like the way my body looked. I felt self-conscious, alone, and isolated most of the time. I was short, not particularly athletic, and a below-average student. I don't believe it was because I wasn't smart enough; I just didn't care and didn't try. The recurring comment from my teachers was, "Robbie doesn't work up to his potential." I wonder how many of our parents got used to seeing comments like this. And the vagueness of the comment left me wondering, "What can I do about it, anyway?" I imagine my parents asked the same question, but we never talked about it.

As an adolescent, body image became more important. I was one of those kids who was uncomfortable taking my shirt off at the pool, and I felt "less than" when compared to others. I didn't think I was as good-looking, I wasn't as thin, I wasn't as tall, and I wasn't a star athlete like some of my friends and classmates.

Pee Wee Grid Champions

Picture above is the Irish football team composed of second, third and fourth graders who captured the Tabernacle Recreation Department Pee Wee football championship with a 9-0 record. The Irish scored 264 points compared to 24 for the opposition as Noble York racked up 25 touchdowns and Steve York 16. The team will be honored at 6:30 p. m. next Friday at an awards banquet in the church dining room. The team: (Front, left to right) Noble York, Bruce Hamilton, Steve York, Scott Norris, Harry Neff and Tom Agnew; (second row, left to right) Hal Bramley, Robert Maynaham, Ed Lacy, Pete Papples, Bill Maroney and George McClure; and (third row, left to right) Coach Gene Norris, Bill Talbeth, Dave Reeves, Bill McClean, Noble Myers and Coach Jerry York.

I was often last to be chosen for team sports and had a short and disappointing career in Pee Wee football and Little League Baseball.

This photo is from the local paper when my Pee Wee football team won the league championship. We won the coveted "Pee Wee Grid Champions" (I'm sure without much help from me). Notice I'm the only one on the team who didn't get a team jersey. They didn't even get my name right in the team roster—apparently, I became *Bill* Maroney. It might seem like a simple mistake, but these *little* experiences along the way imprint deeply and contribute to a boy's feeling lost and invisible.

When I was about ten years old, I found my dad's adult magazine collection and became infatuated with the photographs of beautiful bodies. Being deeply dissatisfied with my own body and feeling like an outsider, along with the typical challenges of puberty and adolescence all boys face at this age, the hook was set for me to start lusting over the beautiful, sexy pictures I saw in the magazines. This was the perfect storm. I was feeling awkward, alone; the hormones had been turned on, and I felt emotionally isolated at home. The combination of loneliness, pain, sexual arousal, and secrecy launched a cycle of unwanted behavior that became repeated into adulthood.

The American Psychological Association reports the largest consumers of pornography are twelve- to seventeen-year-old boys, and most children are first exposed to it between the ages of nine and eleven. As easy as it was for me to find, I can't imagine my mother didn't know about my dad's magazine collection. As a ten-year-old boy, I knew this was something to be kept secret, and by age twelve to thirteen, I had accumulated my own secret library.

One day, my mom and older sister found my collection in my room, but nothing was ever said. There was no discussion with my mother or my father. This was one of the first painful signs of the relational ambivalence in our family. Wondering why no one ever mentioned it, I said to myself, "They either don't care, or they don't know how." My secret magazine collection became something I could control and became a way for me to reclaim a sense of power I felt I had lost in the home with a passive, disconnected father and older, more dominant women.

A father's imprint

Lack of connection and no emotional support in the family contributes to the development of our belief systems about how life and relationships work. When children lack clear and direct communication from important primary people, such as parents, they will write their own script of what's going on in the family. My script said, "Stay off the radar screen, stay invisible, you'll figure it out, but you're on your own."

On my tenth birthday, I got a Daisy Red Ryder BB rifle. I felt like Ralphie in *A Christmas Story* ("I want an official Red Ryder carbine action two-hundred shot range model air rifle"). One day, I hid in the bushes in front of our house, wondering how hard it would be to hit a moving car. As the blue station wagon drove past my house, I leveled the rifle and squeezed the trigger. The furthest thing from my mind was that I would ever hit it, but all of a sudden, the back window of the car exploded into a million pieces. I ran like the wind.

As the driver stopped and backed up to my house, a neighbor who saw what happened turned me in. The man came to the door and explained to my mom and dad what happened, as I stood there in the shadows. Considering I had just blown out the window of his car, this stranger was calm, understanding, and forgiving in a way I couldn't understand. He seemed to know how ten-year-old boys get into these situations. Maybe he had a ten-year-old at home. I quietly wondered to myself, "Why can't my dad be like this?"

Dad made a brief introduction to my mom then motioned toward me with a wrinkled brow, saying, "Of course, you've met *him*." My dad looked at me with the look of disapproval and shame I had become all too familiar with. The strange thing is, we never spoke of it afterward. No one asked what I was thinking or feeling, no processing of feelings or emotion. This is how things were handled in my family, just silent disapproval and shame.

> Every father should remember one day
> his son will follow his example, not his advice.
> (Charles F. Kettering)

This experience and others told me emotions must be dangerous and avoided because nobody talked about them, so they were off-limits. The unspoken message was, identifying and revealing feelings is risky, so be careful what you say about what's going on inside. Isolation is a much safer place. Don't let others in. Safety and belonging are not readily available in this family, and having needs shows weakness. I told myself, "Others won't be there anyway, so don't set yourself up for more pain or waste your effort expressing needs." I eventually wrote another faulty script that would haunt me later in even more destructive ways. I told myself, "Maybe being alone isn't all that bad." Isolation and secrecy were becoming even more attractive.

Young men who grow up with emotionally absent fathers often have trouble with personal and relational areas of their lives. They tend to have low self-esteem; they struggle to establish and maintain intimate relationships and are at greater risk of engaging in antisocial or violent behavior, as well as compromised sexual integrity. I didn't grow up *fatherless* in the sense that my dad was physically present,

56

but he was emotionally absent. A son longs for the affirmation and acceptance of his father. He wants to know his father is pleased with him, not for what he does or does not do but simply because of who he is. This kind of father connection was missing for me.

In his book *The Father Factor*, Stephan Poulter writes, "this fathering style made up approximately 50 percent of nuclear families between 1945 and 1980."[6] It's the kind of dad we saw on *Leave It to Beaver*. It's the dad who is a "good guy," and some would consider him a "good dad." But there's a problem. Although he might frequently be around, he's not emotionally there; he's not present to others around him; he's not attune to the feelings or emotional needs of his family.

The skills to open up emotionally and be vulnerable with feelings are first modeled and learned at home. Children who grow up without these skills not only fail to develop healthy relationships with their fathers, but they also struggle in developing healthy relationships with others. Never learning to recognize or express emotions and never having it modeled in a healthy way at home, these children grow up lacking the skills to be vulnerable with their spouses, their kids, and their friends. This describes my relationship with my dad. As I grew older, got married, and started my own family—and as much as I told myself I wouldn't be like him—these same limitations showed up in my relationships with Roxanne and our children.

When my parents were both in their early forties, my mom got the unexpected news: she was pregnant again. I was twelve years old, and I don't think my parents were planning on this new little surprise. My mother obviously became a preoccupied mom, with a newborn baby girl in addition to her two other children. Adding this pressure to the existing emotional disconnection in my home, I became even more invisible and unseen.

Some people would argue that Bo Jackson was the greatest athlete ever to live. Playing both professional football and baseball, there isn't much more Bo Jackson could have done to excel in athletics.

---

[6]   Stephan Poulter, *The Father Factor* (Prometheus Publishing, 2006).

Yet at the top of his game, he still felt the wound of an emotionally absent father. Bo Jackson revealed this pain in an interview with *Sports Illustrated*:

> My father has never seen me play a football or baseball game. Can you imagine? Here I am, Bo Jackson, one of the so-called premier athletes in the country, and I'm sitting in the locker room and envying every one of my teammates whose dad would come in and talk, have a drink with them after the game. I never experienced that.[7]

The message growing up was "you're on your own"

I started working when I was about twelve years old. I had a paper route, worked in an apple orchard near my home, and worked as a drug store delivery driver when I got my driver's license. The transition from junior high to high school was difficult. I went from a little pond to a huge lake. I felt small and lost. The feeling of invisibility I felt in my family was now being kindled even more in school. This is a time of life when boys and girls compete for attention, acceptance, and affection, and I wasn't getting it, so I found other ways.

By the time I was fourteen years old, I was using drugs. By the time I was fifteen or sixteen years old, I was sexually active, using alcohol when I could get it, and shoplifting. Drugs, sex, and acting out became ways to connect with a group of other like-minded teenagers and reclaim a sense of power and control I didn't feel I had in my life. At this early age, I felt invincible, and I was good at not getting caught. I believed I could get away with almost anything.

Within two years, I would head off to college, where it became even easier to continue my unaccountable, unexamined, and isolated

---

[7] R. Hoffer, "What Bo Knows Now," *Sports Illustrated*, 1995, https://vault.si.com/vault/ 1995/10/30.

life. There was one problem, though; my old habits and brokenness came with me. You see, until we acknowledge the brokenness of our past, it follows us wherever we go. If we don't honestly face and deal with the brokenness and pain in our lives, we will certainly pass it on to others. Dan Allender writes, "Most people want to grow, but the price of growth is pain."[8] At this stage of life, I really wasn't thinking about *growth* or being emotionally healthy, and I was unaware of the pain I would likely pass on to others.

Restless and confused

After two years of college, I quit and moved to another state, but after six months of moving from job to job, getting fired from several jobs, and even trying my hand at dealing drugs with a marijuana farm, I returned home to hopefully finish college. Back in college, I ran into a friend I hadn't seen for over a year, and his life had been surprisingly but noticeably changed.

In my family, we didn't talk about spiritual things. We went to church maybe twice a year—Christmas and Easter—and only if it was convenient and the Indiana weather cooperated. Jesus and stories from the Bible fell in the category of Christian mythology to me, and I never thought of myself as a Christian. In fact, I never thought much about God's being involved in my life at all. Being raised to figure out life on my own and to chart my own course, a line from "Invictus" by William Ernest Henley captured my philosophy of life. The poem ends with the phrase, "I am the master of my fate and the captain of my soul."[9] I determine and control my feelings and my destiny, despite the circumstances. I'm in the driver's seat of my life, and I choose the destination.

This philosophy of life was working okay until it wasn't. The change I noticed in my friend intrigued me. I started questioning if being the "captain of my soul" was working for me. The changed

---

[8] Allender, *To Be Told*.
[9] W. E. Henley, *A Book of Verses* (New York: Scribner & Welford, 1891).

life of a close friend intrigued me enough to launch a quiet search to learn more about Jesus. Over the next several weeks, I read, I asked questions, and I eventually laid down a challenge before God, saying, "God, show me You're real, and I will believe in you." This was my way of saying, "Prove it to me."

Although God appeared to be silent, I was learning a valuable lesson about trust and faith. God doesn't always work the way I want, and I eventually found myself wrestling with overwhelming evidence supporting the claims of Jesus. God had already proven Himself. He didn't need to prove Himself to me beyond what He had already done. I found myself saying, "Okay, God, I need You. I don't understand everything about You, but I will believe in You and trust You to show me who You are." That was a new beginning. I let go of the demand that life work on my terms and gradually started moving toward trusting Him. This lesson in trust would be tested again years later as I wrestled with Him during our marriage struggles.

A pivotal move

I started playing guitar when I was twelve and playing music offered a way to escape the emotional void I felt at home. It seemed like music was the one way I could feel. I started my first rock band in high school, but after becoming a Christian, my music interests shifted to the Christian music of the '70s and '80s.

During my last two years of college, I became heavily involved with a large Christian group on campus, and when I graduated, they hired me as a staff member. Although my parents weren't highly supportive or understanding, I moved from Indiana to Colorado and eventually to California. My original plan was to go overseas and work internationally, but when I learned this organization had music groups traveling around the world, it caught my attention. The thought of traveling and playing music while working with a Christian organization had my name written all over it.

This was a pivotal move and the beginning of a new chapter. Not only was I off on another exciting adventure, but this is also when I met and fell in love with Roxanne. She was unlike any other girl I had dated. She was gorgeous, enthusiastic, caring, talented, sensitive, down-to-earth, and she had an emotional bandwidth way beyond anything I had ever experienced. I was completely taken with her. She was fun loving, she had a warm and inviting personality, and I was immediately drawn to her emotional energy, her spontaneity and enthusiasm. My steadiness and calmness represented something entirely different than she grew up within her chaotic family. In the early phase of a relationship you don't always recognize how the laws of attraction are coming into play; you just know when you are falling in love with someone. In this early stage, we weren't aware of the deeper parts of each other's history and didn't really think it mattered.

When couples pay attention to what's happening in their relationship, they often find the very things they are attracted to in each other become the very things that come between them under pressure. In time, Roxanne's emotional energy, which was once exciting and attractive, became overwhelming for me, and my withdrawal, sarcasm, and isolation became unsafe and overshadowed any virtues of stability and steadiness. Little did we realize at the time how the difference between our emotional "Richter scales" would impact our marriage.

Remember our trailers? We were both still pulling our own trailers packed with the stuff we had been towing for years. We just hadn't yet recognized the impact this baggage would have on our relationship.

What we learned was caught, not taught

Looking back, I'm not sure what I expected or even what I was prepared for when we got married. Based on what I saw in my parents' marriage, my understanding of love and intimacy was seriously flawed. Without good role models or solid foundation for how to genuinely love someone sacrificially, I was floundering, and this became painfully obvious in the years ahead.

I pictured marriage as the place where I would be loved and accepted unconditionally, no longer needing to prove myself, and in many ways, this was true. For the first time, I felt truly loved for who

I was, and I didn't have to earn her love. But I was still haunted by the belief that I was flawed, and my insecurities should remain deeply hidden. I also believed that once I got married and sex was available and permitted without guilt, my sexual appetite would be satisfied. I didn't understand the extent to which my intimacy ignorance was linked to my poor self-image, my false beliefs about love and acceptance, my lack of relational courage, and my misunderstanding of the difference between sex and intimacy.

This is a tough but important journey for most men. Our highly sexualized culture and faulty role models have hijacked our thinking and delivered a tainted message to both men and women about their value, creating distorted views of sex and intimacy. Most of what we learned about sex and intimacy were caught rather than taught. If you ask your husband about his role models growing up, he will likely have difficulty coming up with any. For most men, they were few and inadequate. Looking at role models in our culture we might go to "Sexiest Men Alive" in *People* magazine, advertisements for men's products, actors and famous athletes, or even just to the window displays in your local mall. Beneath the surface, however, these lives don't represent healthy masculinity either.

It's likely your partner developed a worldview of sex and intimacy based on faulty thinking and lousy information. I'll say it again: faulty thinking and lousy information! This toxic combination often creates great distress in a relationship and calls for much more than a makeover or a mere "paint job." Instead, a healthy understanding of true intimacy needs to be redefined, reformed, and restored.

The silent killer

This cultural worldview of sex and intimacy has penetrated all areas of our society. Roxanne and I have worked with men and women in leadership roles in the church and other organizations who struggle in this area yet keep it buried beneath the surface to protect a false image they have worked hard to create. Although I was still not being honest with myself or others about my inner battles, like many others, we found ourselves leading, teaching, and mentoring men and women, but I silently struggled inside to apply in my own marriage what I was teaching others. Our unresolved relationship issues continued to boil beneath the surface. My struggle with sexual integrity continued, our marriage was silently suffering, and the hypocrisy created increasing guilt, secrecy, and shame.

Fearing more pain and rejection, one of the heaviest weights I carried was being unable or unwilling to reveal my fears and insecurities to Roxanne.

Discussion Questions

Chapter 2: When the Past Shows Up

For personal reflection

1. Are there parts of Rob's history you identify with or remind you of your spouse? Which ones?
2. Do you have memories of parents' asking about how you were feeling in a caring and curious way? If not, what did they do during times of stress, loss, or discomfort?
3. In your home, did you feel you were on your own in terms of coping with emotions? What did you do when you were upset?

For group discussion

1. Did you feel free asking for help when you were growing up? If not, what were your conclusions about relationships from what you saw?
2. How do you think Rob's history set him up for problems in his marriage later?
3. Is there a part of Rob's story that helps you understand your mate a little better? What was most helpful?

CHAPTER 3

Broken Thinking

Thoughts have actual physical properties. They are real! They
have a significant influence on every cell in your body...
Teaching yourself to control and direct thoughts in a positive
way is one of the most effective ways to feel better.
—Daniel Amen, *Change Your Brain, Change Your Life*

Roxanne

Rob and I are not unique. Our stories are like so many other couples we've met along the way while counseling. We formed habits of thinking, which turned out to be self-destructive but at the time seemed reasonable. In fact, our thoughts were so common and natural, we hardly noticed them. For instance, I never really noticed how critical I was of myself. The distortions I chose to believe seemed like facts: "I'm not good at this," "If I were more spiritual or more _____, life would be better," "I wish I were a better mom," "My hair is too curly," "My hips are too fat," and on and on.

In his book *Change Your Brain, Change Your Life*,[10] Dr. Daniel Amen calls these thoughts ANTS: Automatic Negative ThoughtS.

---

[10] Daniel G. Amen, *Change Your Brain, Change Your Life: The Breakthrough Program for Conquering Anxiety, Depression, Obsessiveness, Anger, and Impulsiveness* (Crown Books, 1998).

These ANTS form grooves in our brain like well-worn highways, and these roads are toxic and lead to judgmental and critical thinking not only of ourselves but also of others. But where did these ANTS come from? I wish it was easy to just think differently, but it's not. So much of my thinking and brain wiring happened long before I was married, but I didn't see the connection at the time.

My habit of critical thinking and harsh comments leaked out often when Rob's weaknesses played out. The more critical I became of him, the more he wanted to distance himself from me, the more I felt rejected by him, and that became our vicious cycle. Neuroscientists have said the average person has around thirty thousand to fifty thousand thoughts a day, and for most of us, a good portion of these are negative, so the process of change starts at the thought level but doesn't end there, as we will see in later chapters. I came by this bad habit honestly. As a child, I was surrounded by broken thinking, toxic thoughts, and criticism not only from family members but also teachers and friends.

Years later when our marriage became more and more of a struggle, my broken thinking revealed my tendency to focus only on the negative and my broken beliefs. I was looking for someone who would love me in an expressive way and never leave me because I had experienced so much loss and abandonment as a child. As a result, I formed unconscious expectations around that belief. For example, if Rob didn't agree with me on a topic, I saw it as a form of rejection or separation. I would say things like, "We need to be on the same page." He never left me physically, but he left mentally and emotionally.

Because of his drive for significance and desire to prove himself, he became a full-blown workaholic. Realizing I was way down on his list of what was important, I became resentful. Another false thought or belief of mine was "if you loved me, you would just know what I want, and if I need to ask, it's not real." There's nothing wrong with having and expressing desires and reasonable expectations in a marriage, but so many are formed out of distortions from our childhoods, and we don't even know it. I was prone to black-and-white thinking, reading minds, and jumping to conclusions. Rob was more inclined to deny or minimize problems and call it having a positive attitude. Both of us needed to take a good, hard look at our expectations and beliefs and the ANTS rolling around in our heads. What consumes your mind controls your life in so many ways.

The truth is we will all move in the direction of our most dominant thought. Although I was a Christian and believed in Scripture, I also held on to some falsehoods from my upbringing. As I became more aware of the false thinking I carried around and false beliefs I brought into marriage, I became more hopeful I could change. It's such a temptation to think my spouse is the whole problem, and if they would just change, I would be fine. I really believed that. But as I took the time to look at my early history, not to lick my wounds and feel sorry for myself but to honestly look at my beliefs and conclusions I formed, I realized the past is not the past if it invades the present, and for both of us, the past was definitely showing up.

Rob

> We cannot solve our problems with the same
> level of thinking that created them.
>
> —Albert Einstein[11]

When a toxic thought takes over your brain, it's most often due to something that occurred years ago or an event you suspect might happen in the future. It rarely has anything to do with what's actually happening in the present moment. That's another reason why staying in the moment is helpful in short-circuiting the toxic thought process. Negative thoughts come up because of our preoccupation with the past and the future. The past cannot

---

[11] Einstein was quoted to have said something similar to this and it was translated into English, but nowhere did he write this or publish this quote. Public Domain.

be relived, and the future never comes. The present moment is our only reality.

The real impact of broken thinking shows up not only in poor choices but also in our wrong conclusions. I often told myself, "I'm not enough," "I'll never be enough," "I'm a disappointment," or "I should do more," and these negative self-talk messages went deeper than passing or occasional thoughts. Broken thinking took me down a much darker path. Roxanne mentioned how her wrong thinking led to false conclusions, which became false beliefs.

My belief that I didn't measure up started long before I met Roxanne, and in many ways, she paid a price for my distorted thinking and faulty self-talk. During our long journey through nine counselors, one of them asked me, "Why is it that other people have to pay for the pain in your life?" This sounded harsh at the time, but as the question sank in, I accepted the reality. I avoided intense emotions and difficult conversations, which affected others around me. My lack of courage to express or receive strong feelings was certainly an imprint from my upbringing, and my discomfort with conflict clearly showed up in my relationships with others.

As a child, I have no recollection of anyone in my family's resolving conflict in a healthy way. I don't even recall anyone raising their voice or getting angry (which, by the way, is not normal or healthy). Anger and conflict were avoided in my home, and I actually grew up to believe anger was a character flaw. I became judgmental of others who didn't control their temper. You can imagine how well that worked for me in business, marriage, church, etc. I learned to hide weakness, never talk about feelings, and not reveal anything I was too ashamed to talk about. It's not that I wasn't angry, I just learned that I couldn't show it. I developed a false belief that secrets keep you safe, when the truth is, secrets keep you sick.

Roxanne and I have often heard couples say, "I'll take care of myself. You take care of yourself." Clearly, this is not a healthy way to sustain a connected relationship, especially the most intimate kind. Eventually, I questioned where my rules of life came from. What were the lessons I learned as a child that I had written on the stone tablets of my heart and had become the guiding influence for how life should be lived? As many of my false beliefs about how to feel safe and secure came to the surface, the deep roots of my self-protection and self-deception were even more exposed.

The past can't be relived, and the future never comes

The subtle messages I heard growing up were, "Don't dwell on the past," "Get over it," "You'll be fine," "Everything will work out." These messages from childhood followed me into my adult relationships, affecting my ability to recognize or acknowledge any true feelings in the present. When I was first encouraged to consider how my past could influence my life today, I resisted the concept. I was one of those who said, "The past is the past." I didn't have an interest in blaming my parents or reliving things I would rather forget. I couldn't see what good it would do. But my reaction to avoid looking back was to focus more on the future.

I didn't see it at first, but the past was bringing up memories of loss, feelings of shame, regret, and disappointment. I didn't know how to express what I felt around difficult memories and never developed a feeling vocabulary to describe my internal state. No wonder I wanted to avoid that! Thinking only about the unknown outcomes of the future or dwelling on the past that you cannot change are both dangerous places to live.

My tendency was to dwell on the positive side of being future focused—I was more optimistic. I was the guy who said, "It's not that bad." But there was also a downside I had to recognize—I minimized the emotional needs of others and believed things worked out on their own given enough time. It's the lie that says "Time heals all wounds." The future was still ahead of me and something I thought I had control over. The truth is, when living in the future, I focus on things that haven't happened yet, things that might or might not even occur, and things I have little or no control over. When living in the future, I also become preoccupied with worry, fear, and anxiety because uncertain outcomes create instability, and undesirable outcomes create disappointment. In reality, the future is full of unknowns and uncertainty.

On the other hand, ruminating on the past is also dangerous. The past has already happened. I already know those outcomes, and some of them were not so great. Powerful thoughts of regret, shame, disappointment, and guilt poured fuel on the painful memories of things I did, things I said, failures, and when I didn't measure up.

I have to be honest and accept that both the past and the future have an influence on my life, but the past and future must be kept in perspective. Although they both exert a powerful influence, I can't change the past, and I can't control the future. The space between my past and the future is my present reality, which is where I live. My present reality may not always feel peaceful, joyful, or hopeful, but this is where God meets me to provide perspective and comfort. This is where I find freedom from accusations, blame, regret, shame, guilt, and disappointment from things in the past I cannot change. Even though I might experience real emotions of sadness, fear, anger, regret in the present, it's also where I am released from the pain of future outcomes I cannot control. It's where I find hope and peace in the midst of what is sometimes a painful reality. This is what it looks like:

Living in the Past	Living in the Present	Living in the Future
Regret	Accept reality (whatever it is)	Fear
Worry	Contentment	Anxiety
Shame	Perspective	Lack of control
Guilt	Peace	Uncertain outcomes
Disappointment	Comfort	Discomfort
Not enough	Joy	Isolation
Never measure up	Hope	On your own

So how did this impact our marriage? A better future does not mean erasing the past. It's in the present—where you are right now, where God meets you, and where you do the work together of rebuilding, restoration, and repair. Dwelling on my past with regret, shame, guilt, and disappointment while looking to the future with worry, fear, anxiety, and lack of control was exhausting. When I wasn't emotionally available to be present in the moment, communication in our marriage was strained and felt awkward. Being preoccupied with everything *except* the here and now made our conversations shallow and circular. I was so fixated on my own internal battles, I had a hard time listening to Roxanne if she wanted to share a struggle she was having even if it wasn't about me. As you can imagine, this eventually led to fewer and fewer conversations and less openness and vulnerability for both of us.

> I wanted to interrupt this cycle and break
> the pattern, and I knew it would take intentional
> work and effort. I just didn't know how.

Roxanne often characterized my life as I lived on my own private island, doing what I wanted, when I wanted, only taking care of myself. My island was a place where I lived an unexamined, unaccountable life. On my private island, I was in control, and lack of control was too unsettling. This *virtual* island was a safe place where I could hide out and protect the image I worked so hard for others to see. I needed to find a way off the island.

The old way and the new way

Making the choice to embrace change will always bring us to a fork in the road. One path will lead to a new way, while the other keeps us on the old, familiar path. This old, familiar way revealed our broken ways of thinking that focused on doing whatever we could do to make life work. My way of "making life work" was to live on my terms and according to how I defined a "better life," which was usually just another way of saying "an easier life."

When God started renewing and restoring my way of thinking by breaking down my independence and self-sufficiency, I came to my fork in the road. I had to make a choice for a new way, for honesty, for vulnerability, for humility. The starting place was realizing I couldn't fix my life on my own, and I needed God's intervention. The lessons I learned in my family growing up told me I was on my own, and it was up to me to figure out life. For most of my life, I functioned autonomously, leaving little room for influence from anyone else. If things worked out well, I got the credit. If things didn't work out so well, I got the blame. Either way, it was all about me; it was my pride fully in control.

Believing I was in control of every aspect and outcome of my life was a self-centered way of thinking. Letting go of this belief was not easy, but it helped me identify what my deepest need really was: brokenness, repentance, and greater longing for God. Once I honestly acknowledged my broken thinking, my unrealistic expectations and demands, I could pursue things that didn't come naturally, like vulnerability with a community, openness with God, and honesty with myself. Resisting unhealthy ways of pursuing comfort, influence, prestige, and success, which are all rooted in pride, also began to change.

I readily admit I don't understand what it's like to be in a woman's shoes, but I have a pretty good idea what it's like to be in your husband's or partner's shoes. If you are in a relationship with someone who has struggled with sexual integrity or any unwanted sexual behavior, I have compassion for how you have been deeply wounded. My lack of integrity wounded Roxanne. My secrecy, dishonesty, and denial were painful reminders of what she experienced with her mother and touched raw spots in her life regarding trust. When your husband or partner is in the midst of his own journey of healing from sexual integrity issues, he must go through his own process of understanding, acceptance, ownership, responsibility, self-awareness, forgiveness, and recovery.

It might seem difficult to accept the reality that tension and uncertainty are part of a relationship, but rather than being destructive and separating, they can actually create an opportunity for greater trust and connection. This way of thinking values integrity and authenticity rather than self-protection. With new ways of thinking, brokenness over weakness and sin become more important than avoiding vulnerability and holding on to resentment about the wounds inflicted on us by others. We will explore this more when we discuss forgiveness in chapter 5.

My journey is ongoing, and I continue gaining new insight and clarity on how my past influences the present. Connecting the dots on where your broken thinking started and the power it has to affect other areas of your life is vital to your growth.

Roxanne: The Path to Healing

When it comes to thinking and beliefs, awareness always comes first because so much of what we ponder or believe in is almost unconscious. My friend Kay Yerkovich says, "Insight is easy, change is hard." As much as we would like it to be enough, awareness alone isn't the answer. We must take courageous steps.

Studies have shown the most lasting changes come from small and consistent movements and actions. For example, years ago I, used to be a personal trainer. Most people came to me to become fit and lose weight, but if I were to ask those clients their thoughts about how people lose weight, almost all would state the facts: eat less and exercise more. Then why were they coming to me? What prevented them from losing the weight? They were often unaware of what they were thinking and believing that was sabotaging their progress, making it harder to even accomplish small steps. If they thought food was their means to comfort or if they didn't believe they had the will or strength to change, their journey of growth or fitness would be futile.

It's the same with relationships. Noticing my thought process helped me see my broken view of myself and my broken view of Rob. In my thirties, I reached a point of fatigue. I was waiting for Rob to change so I could change. After the first counselor helped me see the impact of my past, I realized I needed to grow and change even if Rob didn't. This was my first stage of growth but certainly not the last. We still languished on for many years as a couple because it wasn't yet a team effort. To forge a truly healthy relationship, we both needed to clean up our side of the street and take responsibility for our own behavior, our own weaknesses, and our faulty beliefs. For a couple to really heal, both of them have to do the work.

Awareness: The first step but not the last

Growth begins with becoming more attentive and aware of your feelings, thoughts, and behaviors. Increasing your self-awareness involves taking an honest inventory of your beliefs and where they originated. Growth involves self-examination of what motivates you to do the things you do; it requires asking tough questions and being open to your blind spots.

Rob and I both believed we were right in our positions, but in fact, we were both wrong about so many things. We both underestimated and often entirely dismissed the impact of our upbringing, so awareness was a slow process of connecting the dots of what happened in our pasts *and* the conclusions we came to. This process required courage because it's much easier to stay fixed with a false assumption that the world should change rather than I need to change. I was open to looking at my flaws but still nervous about whether anything would change because of my lingering belief that "a leopard doesn't change its spots."

That was a belief I needed to recognize and change. Because our beliefs are the foundation for nearly everything we do, more will be said about this in the coming chapters.

A growth mindset versus a fixed mindset

Most people like to think of themselves as positive and open-minded. They say they are accepting of change and have a growth mindset. But the way they respond to a few statements often reveals something quite different. In their book *Switch: How to Change Things When Change Is Hard*,[12] Chip and Dan Heath ask readers to write down whether they agree or disagree with each of these statements:

1. You are a certain kind of person, and not much can be done to really change.

---

[12] Chip Heath and Dan Heath, *Switch: How to Change Things When Change Is Hard* (Penguin Random House, 2010).

2. No matter what kind of person you are, change is always possible.
3. You can do things differently, but the important parts of who you are really don't change.
4. You can always change basic things about the kind of person you are.

Readers who agreed with statements 1 and 3 have what they call a "fixed mindset." This is the mindset that says, "I am who I am and probably won't change much." You believe who you are, and your ability to change is static. You might believe you can get a little better or worse in a few areas, but your basic belief is this is how you are wired. All too often, we hear one (or sometimes both) partners say, "This is just the way I am, get used to it." This is a sad and selfish way of saying, "Don't expect me to change." Someone with a fixed mindset tends to avoid challenges and feels threatened by negative feedback out of a fear of failure or fear of weakness being exposed.

But readers who agree with statements 2 and 4 tend to have more of a "growth mindset." A growth mindset believes your abilities are like muscles that can be developed and strengthened with practice. Let's face it, good relational skills are hard to learn. Successful friendships, partnerships, family relationships, and marriages all take work and effort. With a growth mindset, you are willing to accept more challenges and take a chance despite the risk of failure. You don't become paralyzed by thinking failure is fatal. With a growth mindset, you are willing to stretch yourself, take a risk that might be outside your comfort zone, accept feedback, and take a long-term view.

A "fixed mindset" will always limit your growth. Avoiding change, being closed to learning something new or something different, resisting input and feedback from others, and protecting yourself from failure only keeps you stuck. In contrast, having a growth mindset assumes we accept that we are beginners when we learn a new skill but know there is potential of getting better. Letting go of our fixed mindset and adopting more of a growth mindset, especially when we were struggling, helped us become more flexible, patient, and understanding with each other.

Challenge your beliefs

Shifting from a "fixed mindset" to a "growth mindset" was difficult, especially when I was convinced I was right. But as I openly asked myself questions like, "Is there another way to see this?" or "Is this way of thinking even biblical?" or "am I making an assumption here?" the holes in my perspective became clear. I was often guilty of writing a narrative in my head and arriving at conclusions without ever checking them out. I can't easily stop a thought from going through my head, but I can stop it from becoming a belief. There's an old quote attributed to Martin Luther: "You can't stop birds from flying overhead, but you can stop them from nesting in your hair."

Thinking about this one day, I made a list of twelve of my personal values. Values are the important beliefs or standards we live by, and we often become judgmental of those who don't live consistent with these same important beliefs and standards. Then I asked myself, is this value from God, or is it negatively influenced by one or both of my parents or someone else? To my surprise, most were from my parents, Eddie and Gloria. For example, honesty is one of my highest core values, and I really struggled with anyone who was not completely honest. But I was hypersensitive in this area because my mother rarely told the truth. Is honesty a good value? Yes, of course, but my energy and intolerance were directly tied to a mom who was broken in this area of her life.

As I recognized the connection to my history and past wounds, my emotional reactions decreased and lost their power when listening to someone stretching or altering the truth. I was then able to be less reactive in my response to someone who wasn't truthful because I was no longer tapping into a wound from my past.

Another false belief I had was that my sins weren't as bad when compared to Rob or others. Although the *consequences* of what we do may differ greatly, if we look at it from God's perspective, it is the motive of the heart that's all important. For example, Jesus leveled the playing field in the Sermon on the Mount in Matthew 5 when He compared insults and anger to murder.

> You have heard that it was said to our ances-
> tors, Do not murder, and whoever murders will
> be subject to judgment. But I tell you, everyone
> who is angry with his brother or sister will be
> subject to judgment. Whoever insults his brother
> or sister, will be subject to the court. (Matthew
> 5:21–22 CSB)

While "don't murder" seems like an easy standard to follow, Jesus made a shocking connection between thoughts and actions. God's intent behind the sixth commandment goes far beyond *just* not killing people. It's meant to be applied at the deepest levels of our thoughts and feelings toward every single person.

Wait, what? If the attitude of my heart can be compared to murder, then I was guilty. I thought Rob's sin of keeping secrets, stretching the truth, and avoiding was much worse than my quiet contempt, resentment, and secrets about my spending habits. I had to humbly acknowledge my own faults and internal attitudes and come off my pedestal. We both had stuff to work on, but they showed up in different forms of brokenness. Thank goodness God is gentle and welcoming of each of us. Nothing surprises Him, and no sin is too great for Him to forgive.

Gaze and Glance

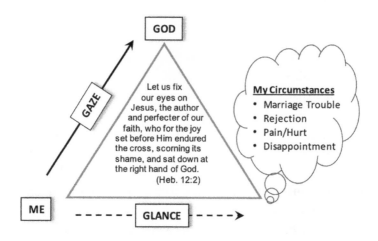

During our struggles, I was often hyperfocused on our relationship and how we were falling short. I still can do this when I'm struggling with my health, one of our kids, or any number of other hard circumstances.

Years ago, I saw this diagram that revealed my tendency to *gaze* on my fear and troublesome circumstances, and only *glance* toward God with a quick prayer now and then. But to grow in faith and have any peace despite our trials, the opposite is necessary. Throughout Scripture, God invites us to *gaze* at His character, His goodness, His power and *glance* at our circumstances. When I get this backward, my circumstances become huge, and God becomes very small, leading me to rely on myself more than Him.

> Trust in the Lord with all your heart, and do
> not rely on your own understanding; in all your
> ways know him, and he will make your paths
> straight. (Proverbs 3:5–6 CSB)

From these verses, it appears that if I gaze (trust and rely) on God, He will make everything easy or right according to what I expect or want. But I believe these verses speak more about our internal journey with Him. Sometimes my circumstances change; other times, He changes me.

As I look in the rearview mirror, many of the trials I've faced make sense, and I see they were His means of liberating me. I still don't understand some of the ways He works in my life, and I will have to trust Him with that mystery until I see Him face to face. As hard as it is sometimes, when I catch myself fixated on problems, trials, disappointments, how messed up the world is, I make a conscious effort to change my focus. It's not that I don't see or pray about those issues, I just put more of my energy in marinating in who God is and how much He cares.

Reacting versus responding

> Between stimulus and response there is a space. In that space is our power to choose our response. In our response lies our growth and our freedom.[13]

Let's talk about reacting versus responding. These words are often used synonymously, but to me there's a world of difference. A *reaction* happens in an instant. It's when our unconscious mind and gut takes over and are driven by beliefs, biases, and prejudices. When we say or do something "without thinking," that's our unconscious mind running the show. Our reactions are based in the moment, and no thought is given to long-term effects of what we do or say. A reaction might turn out okay but often is something we regret later.

On the other hand, a *response* is more thoughtful, comes more slowly, and uses both our instincts and our conscious mind. When we respond, we take into consideration not only our own well-being but also the well-being of those around us. A thoughtful response weighs the long-term effects and stays connected with our core values. The

---

[13] A. Pattakos, *Prisoners of Our Thoughts: Viktor Frankl's Principles for Discovering Meaning in Life and Work* (Berrett-Koehler Publishers, 2010).

point is that the more reactive we are, the less empowered we are. We operate from underlying assumptions and beliefs we may not even be aware of, resulting in communication breakdowns. Responding is communicating in a way that doesn't create barriers to the other person's understanding our perspective and yet doesn't throw down the gauntlet, creating a challenging and emotionally unsafe situation bound to result in a defensive stance in the other person.

Although correcting our thoughts and beliefs is important, it's also about being sensitive and attentive enough to think about what we say before we say in order to have a love-focused response. There is great value correcting our thoughts because beneath those thoughts are beliefs that are not healthy or not even true. Many of these beliefs are developed with an immature understanding of life. We often incorporate them at a gut-reaction preverbal stage and often without examining them with adult understanding and maturity. As we learn to respond rather than react, we ask, "What is really true here and now? Am I reacting out of old habits, old patterns, old scripts and wounds, or am I responding in a way that is loving, understanding, kind, redemptive, and offering the grace and hospitality I've received and continue to receive?"

As we think about reacting versus responding, consider the value of these distinctions not only in how we relate to others but also in how we relate to ourselves. This can be another way of recognizing the lies and truths we tell ourselves about ourselves. When I find myself reacting, do I move quickly to toxic thoughts and beliefs about myself that are untrue? Do I ruminate over something I said and tell myself more lies about myself? When I slow down and take time to respond from a more thoughtful place, am I able to see more clearly, sort out truth from lies, and not make negative assumptions and conclusions? Again, when we respond, we take into consideration not only the well-being of those around us but our own well-being as well. We weigh the long-term effects and stay connected with our core values.

Perspective

As Astronaut Neil Armstrong stood on the surface of the moon, looking at planet earth, he gained a renewed appreciation for the importance of perspective. These are the words Neil Armstrong spoke at that moment:

> It suddenly struck me…that tiny pea, pretty and blue, was the Earth. I held up my thumb and shut one eye, and my thumb blotted out the planet Earth. I didn't feel like a giant. I felt very, very small.

It's amazing how something as small as our thumb can block out the entire planet Earth from our field of vision. Yet how often does our unwillingness to put ourselves in another's shoes keep us from hearing, and we block out what they are saying? Perspective changes everything, like blocking out our view of the Earth with something as small as our thumb. Changing our perspective is like changing the window through which we view the world. When we change how we view the world, we change how we feel about it.

But the window through which we see often gets clouded. We see the world not as it is but as molded by the individual peculiarities of our minds, our own experience, and perspective. An old saying of unknown origin describes how each of us look through the eyes of our prejudices, preconceived notions, our unclean windows. Hence, it can be the most difficult thing in the world for us to broaden our vision to see as others see.

> We do not see things as they are. We see things as we are.[14]

---

[14] Rabbi Shemuel ben Nachmani, as quoted in the Talmudic tractate Berakhot (55b).

Our shift in perspective came when we were able to try on each other's views with curiosity and without defensiveness. As we developed a measure of empathy for each other's history, we gradually cleaned our windows of perspective, thus helping us to see and hear one another.

In the next chapter, we will look at how our perspective affects our self-image and the dangers of reactivity and defensiveness.

Discussion Questions

Chapter 3: Broken Thinking

For personal reflection

1. Which way do you lean in terms of your thoughts? Are they more positive or negative? Track your thoughts in a journal for a few days. Write out these thoughts and see what patterns you identify.
2. What do you see about your own broken thinking and beliefs from Rob's thoughts and struggles?
3. Are you waiting for your spouse to change before you change? What part of that belief may you need to adjust?
4. List twelve core values (strong beliefs and morals you live by) and then ask if any of them were formed due to the absence of that value, a negative message from one or both of your parents, or if it is a value you believe is directly from God. Many people find at least half of their strong beliefs come from the absence of a value or a negative influence.

For group discussion

1. Ask yourself if you have a growth or a fixed mindset. Where did this start, and how can you move from fixed to growth? Write out your thoughts and share if you are in a trusted group.
2. Look over the Gaze and Glance diagram. Talk about what you usually do when you are in a trial or hard circumstance. Most of us gaze at our circumstances. What are some baby steps that can help shift your focus?
3. Read over Hebrews 12:1–2. What do you hear that's encouraging about shifting your focus?

> Therefore, since we also have such a large cloud of witnesses surrounding us, let us lay

aside every hindrance and the sin that so easily ensnares us. Let us run with endurance the race that lies before us, keeping our eyes on Jesus, the pioneer and perfecter of our faith. For the joy that lay before him, he endured the cross, despising the shame, and sat down at the right hand of the throne of God. (Hebrews 12:1–2 CSB)

4. Share any new discoveries about yourself from listing your core values with your group. How many are a reaction to what you did or did not see growing up?

5. How would you or your situation be different if instead of praying (or begging) God to change things, you practiced more prayers of thanks for who God is and His love, care, and power?

CHAPTER 4

Broken Self-Image

There is an old Hebrew saying: "God is not a
kindly old uncle; he is an earthquake." This is great
news for those of us struggling with unanswered
prayer, because a kindly old uncle can merely smile
at things that an earthquake can actually shift.

—John Kirvan, *God Hunger: Discovering the Mystic in All of Us*

Define yourself radically as one beloved
by God. This is the true self. Every
other identity is an illusion.

—Brennan Manning, *Abba's Child*

Roxanne

I don't think I could have described my self-image as a child other
than a vague notion I didn't measure up, and I certainly doubted
my lovability. I know no one comes through childhood without
some form of pain and suffering, being bullied, cast aside from the
in crowd, or for some of us, much worse. But as I've said before,
it's about the *conclusions* we come to about ourselves more than the
events.

I was abused and certainly neglected as a child, but I vividly recall one event that left a deep mark. I was seven years old and overheard a heated conversation between my parents just prior to their divorce. My mother sounded sober, and they were arguing over how to divide things up as part of the divorce: the house, the cars, and the kids.

When the topic came to what to do with Roxanne, they each said, "You take her," "No, you take her." I was being tossed about like a hot potato, and it was clear neither of them wanted me. I believed my father really preferred his sons, and my mother was too sick to care for me. The truth is, I didn't want to go with her anyway. What I heard was that neither of them wanted me, and based on their comments, I concluded I must not be worth much. This was a hard realization at seven years old. I concluded it was better to stay invisible and not make waves because my seven-year-old mind told me I could be discarded if I was too much trouble.

My parents were confused people. I believe they loved me the best they knew how at the time, but based on their actions, I didn't feel I was valuable to them. This conclusion can cause someone to work harder to prove their worth—earn good grades, find an area to excel, and basically cause no trouble—or go the opposite direction and totally rebel out of anger. To survive in my home, I chose to stay invisible and just remain nice.

Due to my insecurity and self-doubt, this showed up in the early years of my marriage, mostly by being agreeable and going with the flow. But around the twenty-year mark as I felt more invisible and unappreciated, I thought, *The heck with this.* I decided to find my own path and speak up, but it was not coming from a secure place. My self-image was still stuck in false beliefs from what I'd experienced.

Our parents *authored* the first ten to fifteen years of our lives, but after we become Christians, our challenge is to allow God to *author* or have authority over the remainder of our lives. I knew how Scripture repeatedly said how much He loved me; I knew the verses, but when it came to my feelings and reactions, you wouldn't know it.

I determined my worth based on what people thought of me or how they treated me, never mind what Scripture says.

Rob and I were both looking for each other's approval to feel secure because we received little approval or affirmation growing up. Fear of people's disapproval, judgment, or rejection extended beyond our marriage. Tim Keller writes,

> There are God substitutes, the first being human approval. The fear of man is a snare. If we look to human beings more than to God for our worth and value, we will be trapped by anxiety, by an over-need to please, by the inability to withdraw from exploitative relationships, by the inability to take criticism, and by a cowardice that makes us unable to confront others.[15]

In some ways, Rob and I shared the same haunting insecurity, but it expressed itself in different ways. In our efforts over the years to repair our brokenness, we saw nine different counselors, sometimes alone and sometimes together. They listened compassionately and offered practical advice—like listen better, have a date night—but depending on how ugly of a picture each of us would paint, some went as far as recommending divorce.

I wasn't convinced I had grounds for divorce. I did not want the kids to suffer, so I figured I was left to find my own way in life without him. We still lived together, giving the appearance of a "happy couple," but the canyon was growing wider between us. Our broken self-images were pulling us apart, and we didn't know what to do about it.

One night, we had a conversation while watching a news story about a shooting that took place in a grocery store near our home. I told Rob I was sure if we had been there, he would have jumped in front of me and taken a bullet for me, but I wasn't sure he was

---

[15] Tim Keller, *God's Wisdom for Navigating Life* (Viking, 2017).

willing to live for me or if he had the courage to change for me. You see, which is harder? To jump in front of a bullet in a momentary act of heroism or do the hard work of growing and developing a strong, healthy marriage for the next forty years? I believed he would *die* for me; I just wondered, would he *live* for me? But living "for me" also meant living "for himself."

We are called by God to love our partners, but no matter how well Rob loved me, no one could fill the hole my parents created. No human has the power to provide the kind of security only God can provide. We all carry our baggage from our past into the present. Rob grew up without much affection or affirmation, so he was eager for my affirmation. What he really wanted was approval from someone important to him and a good grade to feel better about himself. While we should offer encouragement to our partners, when there is a giant black hole, we will never be able to fill it.

So much has been written about the difference between genders, such as *Men Are from Mars, Women Are from Venus*, and the sexes are different to be sure. But not everything can be explained away by gender difference alone, and if it were, we couldn't do anything about it. Much of what Rob and I struggled with, what we expected and sometimes demanded from each other, came from our broken self-images. I struggled with low self-worth, insecurity, and abandonment. Rob struggled with shame, rejection, and performing to earn love and acceptance, and neither of us recognized the powerful hold this had on our lives and how it showed up in our marriage.

I was ready to do whatever it took to experience something new, not just in our marriage but in me. Learning to see myself for who I really am and accepting who God says I am was a big part of my journey of healing and recovery. But as mentioned before, Rob was on his own journey of recovery and repair.

Rob: Making the Choice to Change

There's an old joke that asks, "Where does an eight-hundred-pound gorilla sit?" The answer, "Anywhere he wants." Shame was an invisible eight-hundred-pound gorilla I carried on my back. Basically, when he's on your back, he's in charge, and when he's on your back, you're going to sit wherever he wants to sit.

At the core of shame and its real power over our lives is how elusive it can be. There are many words we use for shame like embarrassment, humiliation, exposed, disgraced, among others. But shame has deep roots and is often confused with guilt because guilt seems easier to define. At the risk of oversimplifying, guilt says, "I've done something wrong," while shame says, "There's something wrong with me." Shame is typically described as something I *feel*, and the powerful, deep impact lies in my emotional response to whatever events or circumstances triggered that feeling. Starting with self-accusation, shame moves from "there's something wrong with me" to "I am not enough" and leads to a deeper, more toxic *belief* that "I am unable or powerless to change." Shame is a deep feeling of inadequacy.

Our beliefs inform our thoughts and feelings in powerful ways. When viewing shame solely through the lens of "I am not enough," "there's something wrong with me," "I am bad," or "I don't matter," it still falls short of the full picture. The power of shame is tied more to what I feel rather than what I think, and the root system of shame is supported by the beliefs I embrace. No wonder my efforts to restructure my thinking fell short of an effective solution.

Don't misunderstand me here; confronting and changing negative thought patterns are an important intervention, but when challenged to confront negative thoughts simply with a different way of thinking, the same residual feelings that give energy to the thought in the first place remain: "I don't have what it takes." Simply telling myself I *shouldn't* be ashamed only reinforced the shame. This is the elusive nature of shame. It's deeper than we think, and it's rooted in what we sense, what we feel, what we tell ourselves about ourselves. It's rooted in our beliefs.

You may have heard it said, "Hurt people hurt people," but we can also say, "shamed people shame people." Guilt says, "*I made* a mistake." Shame says, "*I am* a mistake." In my family, there was a subtle and sometimes not-so-subtle message of not being worth loving or being unlovable, and I definitely felt invisible, creating wounds of insignificance, incompetence, and impotence. Beneath my wound of insignificance, I asked, "Do I matter?" Underneath my wound of incompetence, I asked, "Am I adequate and capable?" And feeding my wound of impotence, I wrestled with, "Am I helpless and powerless?"

Shame fueled my harmful habits and isolation, but isolation seemed attractive to me because it felt so controllable. I could choose to live alone on my own self-created island where I decided if and when anyone else could join me. But as the layers of self-protection and defensiveness peeled away, I realized I really wasn't alone; that eight-hundred-pound gorilla was still with me, and getting him off my back was up to me.

One of my major fears was that life would pass me by, leaving me insignificant, invisible, and powerless. These fears played in the background of my mind over and over and haunted me. Growing up in a family where love and acceptance was earned rather than freely and unconditionally given, I organized my life to make sure I mattered, that I was valued, and that I was needed.

Secrets keep us sick

It's been said that "secrets keep us safe," but the truth is secrets keep us sick. I focused a lot of energy and effort on keeping my insecurities hidden. As a result, I became a full-blown workaholic. My self-worth became tightly linked to being seen as competent and capable. Like an actor auditioning for a starring role, the relentless roots of workaholism grew deeper as my quest to be recognized and chosen for positions of increased responsibility and visibility took center stage. Although I often felt like a phony, I was still driven to maintain the image of success and keep secret how deeply I truly felt I was falling short. I eventually reached the point where I believed this had gone on too long, but I still didn't see how I could come clean and be honest about how incapable I really felt.

Protecting my fragile self-image was exhausting, as well as taking a toll on our marriage. As opportunities for new positions of leadership and influence came my way, I worked hard to hide my insecurities so others wouldn't see just how much I felt I was over my head. Seeking bigger and better challenges, I was like a moth drawn to a flame.

After ten years of marriage and over a decade in ministry, I was now doubting some of the choices I had made and feeling unsure what I should be doing with my life. My friends and peers were entering the second decade of their professional careers, and I was still trying to figure out what to do with my life and worried about how to make a living to support our growing family. Feeling disillusioned and without direction, I convinced Roxanne we should leave the ministry. We were living in California at the time, and I accepted a job in my hometown of Indianapolis. Feeling I was behind the pack and pressured to make up for lost time, I entered the business world as an anxious, driven young man with something to prove. This move launched a series of career moves that had a deep and long-lasting ripple effect.

Over the next ten years as I chased my elusive vision of success, I moved our family across the country four times, and I changed jobs six times. Roxanne was not always 100 percent supportive of each of these moves, but she buried her reservations and followed my lead. My attention was misplaced on what seemed best for me rather than what was best for our marriage and our family.

As my wandering continued, my internal struggle intensified. Moving to a new city or finding a new job not only failed to satisfy but actually magnified the feelings of failure and that the elusive success I was chasing would always be just out of reach. The seeds of "not being enough" had been planted long ago as a child, and now, like a well-watered plant, these roots were growing deeper.

Several years later as I sat in a counselor's office, he helped me recognize I needed to get rid of the eight-hundred-pound gorilla. He looked me in the eye and said, "Rob, I would love to help you, but I can't do battle with an eight-hundred-pound gorilla. I'll never win that fight." He then followed up with, "And Roxanne can't tackle this beast either, so don't make it her fight."

At this point, some dark coping mechanisms that had been buried for a long time came back to the surface. I was facing career dissatisfaction, family pressures, relocations, and a growing marital divide, and my unhealthy ways of managing stress were being even more exposed. In the darkness of the struggle, compromised sexual integrity became an acceptable form of stress relief.

Although the behavior itself seemed like the real problem, I discovered it was only a symptom of a deeper longing in my heart and revealed how poorly I was managing the chaos in my life. Being honest about an unhealthy relationship with pornography was the beginning (although I don't believe a *healthy* relationship with pornography is possible). I had to get beneath the symptoms and deal with the real issues: how I viewed myself, keeping secrets, the power of shame, how I dealt with stress, my view of God, and a host of other deeper issues.

When the canary stops singing

Knowing how to be together and how to be apart is essential in a healthy relationship. Feeling secure enough to stand on our own, to trust and motivate ourselves, as well as knowing there is someone else we feel safely connected to and someone we can lean on are important. It was so much easier for Roxanne and me to feel connected when we agreed and when our goals and needs aligned. It was easy for me to express myself when there was little risk of conflict. But when we were stressed, irritable, and tired, our ability to balance separateness and togetherness was truly tested. My anxiety and impatience increased when we disagreed or wanted different things. Different opinions and perspectives threatened our security in the relationship, and our unhealthy patterns of relating to each other kicked into high gear.

At the extreme ends, some people cannot tolerate either being too alone or too close; either one creates discomfort and pain. When my emotional well-being was heavily dependent on Roxanne's emotional state, my stress increased, and I became more tense, thinking I was expected to *fix* something. In this anxious state, I wanted the uneasy feelings and tension to go away more than I wanted to feel more connected to Roxanne. Pushing feelings aside never made them go away; they just got buried deeper. I had ignored my feelings for so long that even if I could unbury them, I didn't have language for them.

There is a familiar account of how canaries were used in coal mines to detect the presence of carbon monoxide. The little bird's rapid breathing rate, small size, and high metabolism compared to the miners caused these fragile small birds to succumb before the miners ever became aware of the elevated carbon monoxide levels. When the canary was found in the bottom of its cage, it gave the miners time to get out of the mine. For over seventy-five years, these little birds acted as their early-warning system.

In our relationship, Roxanne was the canary. She was the early-warning system to tell me if something was not right. I was so unfamiliar with recognizing, understanding, and responding to the emotional well-being of someone else that I didn't even notice when the canary was struggling at the bottom of the cage. When I finally noticed she was on life support and that we weren't in a good place, my hypervigilance kicked in to try harder, make promises, and make some white-knuckled, last-ditch effort to change. But eventually, I would drift back to relying on the canary to be the warning light, to give signs of life, and to let me know if it was still safe to be down in the mine shaft. She became the barometer of how *we* were doing. She determined our level of closeness or separateness.

Although my family was not a threatening or abusive home like Roxanne's, I did not have role models that inspired personal confidence, security, and courage. I doubted myself in most areas of my life. I didn't learn to be open, vulnerable, or trusting. To communicate assertively and confidently in an intimate relationship takes courage, and I never saw this growing up. I didn't have healthy models of courage that comes from self-acceptance, enabling me to value and honor feelings and needs and risk criticism or rejection when voicing those feelings and needs. Giving a voice to our feelings also means believing we deserve love and that we are comfortable receiving love. No wonder when we bring these underdeveloped skills into marriage, the stage is set for a huge emotional intimacy gap. Why would someone waste time pursuing an emotionally unavailable person who pushes them away whenever they move toward them to try to meet their needs?

Roxanne was usually the first to voice concerns about our relationship. She would be the first to initiate a conversation about our lack of connection and how we were drifting apart. When the gap was growing between us, I was reluctant to open up the conversation because I thought it meant another discussion about where I was falling short and not meeting her needs. In my mind, these conversations became another painful reminder of my failure and inadequacy. When she would say, "We need to talk," my stomach went into a knot. I could hear the canary whispering, "Hey, something's happening with the air in here, and I'm having trouble breathing." In those moments I found myself thrown back into seventh grade, walking into class only to find out we're having a pop quiz, and I hadn't cracked the book all year. Just like the seventh-grade test, I had already failed this conversation with Roxanne before it even started, and I missed seeing the canary gasping for air.

Rather than being present and listening to her heart as she shared feeling sad, disconnected, and alone, I heard judgment and criticism of how I was falling short, I was failing, I was not enough, and I was missing the mark. If she shared anything difficult or painful about our relationship, I would immediately shut down, take it personally, become defensive, and feel blamed. I would go into a "good/bad split," where everything was either all good or all bad and there was little room for middle ground. On the outside, I rarely expressed anger, but on the inside, a storm was raging as I tried to hide my anger and resentment of feeling judged. Even worse, I had almost given up entirely on being able to identify and express my feelings and needs appropriately.

When safety, security, and trust are compromised, intimacy is lost

With my fragile self-image still calling the shots, I concealed how I really felt to avoid making waves. If I thought my words would be hard to hear, sound too critical, be misunderstood or judged, I couldn't be honest with Roxanne. When there isn't enough security and trust to be honest, true intimacy is compromised, and the relationship remains on thin ice. This was our pattern. This was our dance for years.

I never thought I would face deciding between being happily married or miserably coexisting, but the bonds we create are often a reflection of the bond our parents modeled. In my case, my parents were compatible roommates and coexisted for over sixty years. I know there were long seasons of dissatisfaction in their relationship, but they stuck it out and stayed together. Although I didn't see this as the model for a healthy marriage, it did introduce an option: maybe you can be unhappy roommates—just stick it out, stay together no matter how unfulfilling it becomes.

Roxanne's model for marriage was entirely different. Her trust in others and her belief that relationships can last a lifetime was damaged very early. Roxanne's parents were both married four times, and their marriage was destroyed by her mother's alcoholism. She came into our marriage with an option entirely different from mine: marriage often doesn't work out, people leave, and it ends in divorce.

Couples often replicate the patterns of behavior they observed and learned from their parents. When the marriage between Mom and Dad was difficult, if childhood was difficult, these couples often enter marriages of their own that also become difficult. When Roxanne and I met and fell in love, everything seemed wonderful. And it was wonderful…up to the point where it started not being so wonderful. It's not uncommon to fall in love with someone and project your hopes and dreams onto the other person, but much of this projection is about the things we wanted and hoped for but didn't get in childhood. This is why the real work begins with honesty about what we saw, what we heard, and what we experienced and acknowledging the imprint of our history on our present relationships. It takes awareness and courage to say, "Maybe a lot of these difficulties I'm having aren't because there's something wrong with my partner. Maybe I'm projecting unrealistic expectations that don't have anything to do with my partner but are more about my own history."

My healing journey could not be dependent on changing some-one else. I had to take ownership of myself and where I needed to grow. It's moving backward to go forward by letting go of pain, regret, anger, resentment, and entitlement from the past. This means feeling the pain of being left alone, not being loved freely and uncondition-ally, acknowledging my anger, and forgiving the rejection I felt from important people in my life who could have loved me differently. Only then was I able to move forward in the process of healing and renewal.

Roxanne: Our Path to a Healthier Self-Image

My view of God and how I view myself significantly influence all my relationships, including marriage. Many people believe, as did I, their ability to make someone happy makes them more lovable or valuable. In my attempt to secure love from Rob or my kids, I wanted their affirmation to confirm how important I was to them. But this is chasing the wind, especially with children, who switch from being pleased to being perturbed in a moment depending on whether Mom answers *yes* or *no*.

How I viewed God—or rather, how I thought He viewed me—was still under the shadow of feeling unimportant to Him. I still looked for affirmation of my value and worth more from the people around me rather than from an all-loving God. This is as self-cen-tered as the person who demands others to grant all their desires. It appears to be "others focused" and more giving and noble, but in either case, the focus of attention becomes *getting*, and God becomes secondary or merely useful.

I knew my real worth and value was from God, but since I strug-gled with this, I still put too much weight on what others thought. As I grew in this area, I didn't rely on feedback from others with the same weight I used to, freeing me to examine my motives. I noticed how often my giving had "strings attached," even if the actions looked the same. It's not that I don't ask for assurance now and then, like when I've had a hard day, feel fat, or insecure; rather, it's moving step-by-step away from finding all my worth in the assurance of others.

Healthy relationships need to go back and forth. They need to give and receive. We wanted to be sensitive to each other's wants, desires, and needs. Rob was not good at asking for anything (remember, he valued being completely independent). Part of his growth journey was to rewrite the old scripts that told him, "Don't bother asking for anything. No one will be there anyway." Little by little, he started taking the risk of asking for what he wanted to rewrite this false belief.

We remained emotionally ignorant for years, causing me to struggle because so many of my prayers went unanswered. Year after year, I begged and pleaded with both God and Rob for some ray of hope, but we remained stuck. I didn't always see it at the time, but God was working in us. He was gradually shifting our thinking and how we related to each other, not like one massive earthquake (although sometimes He does) but in small tremors. Many of these movements were subtle and almost unnoticeable. I wanted God to snap His finger and change us, making us instantly see what needed to change, to want the right things and experience a different relationship. I see now how He was transforming us slowly, not always to my liking or in my timing but creating lasting change.

You might ask, "If my self-image is somewhat distorted, what effect does this have on my marriage? Why take the time and effort to work on this?" In our case and with many other couples, broken self-image is a big source of oversensitivity, insecurities, triggers, and reactivity. As a result, we ping-ponged off each other's broken self-view, making it nearly impossible to hear and see each other or resolve our conflicts.

Our particular pattern was rarely explosive. Instead, we had circular conversations, causing us to become defensive and concluding the other was blaming or shaming and at fault. Following these interactions, we would pull away and avoid each other altogether for prolonged periods of time to lick our wounds, get angry, become resentful, feel sorry for ourselves—you name it. Put that song on repeat for twenty-five years, and it's a miracle we didn't throw in the towel sooner after dancing that way for so long, although I wanted to many times.

We thought the answer to our broken self-images was to love ourselves more, be positive and confident because "God doesn't make junk," but that's only partly true. Toxic and negative thoughts need to be rewritten. But when the opinions and acceptance of others took center stage, we were never free to be our true selves. Instead of believing the truth of what God said about us, we were striving to get affirmation and acceptance from one another, like two ticks without a dog, sucking the blood from each other. We weren't able to love freely when stuck in this pattern. We couldn't love ourselves or each other. Rather than being genuine and authentic, we lived out of what some have called our *shadow* or our "fake selves," the ones we created to be loved. Brennan Manning calls this false self the imposter. Manning writes,

> While the imposter draws his identity from past achievements and the adulation of others, the true self claims identity in his/her beloved-ness to God.[16]

Gradually, we saw how emotional health and spiritual maturity are inseparable. It is not possible to be spiritually mature while remaining emotionally immature; the two go hand in hand. Although we spent a lot of time learning about the Bible and theology, in contrast, we spent little time understanding and maturing our inner selves.

So how are we to align ourselves closer to God's perspective and how He sees us instead of the beliefs written by our families of origin or the scripts we have written ourselves?

Integrate the good and the bad

Take a moment and think about describing yourself, not in terms of your occupation, gender, religion, children, or the things you do. Stop reading and ask yourself the question, who am I? For

---

[16] Brennan Manning, *Abba's Child* (NavPress, 1997).

most of us, this is a hard question when we take out our accomplishments, achievements, or what we do. But many of us haven't spent much time pondering how God sees us, not really. At the end of the day, I am more bothered by the snarky remarks from a stranger in the grocery store than I am encouraged by how God describes me.

The good news/bad news is that we are all worthy, valuable, *and* broken and in need of a Savior. We are all self-absorbed, wanting our own way *and* wanting to love and be loved. We are born valuable and reflect the image of God *and* flawed *and* prone to sin. It's not one or the other; it's all. Some churches we attended over the years emphasized one over the other. Some emphasized God's love and acceptance; others stressed we are sinners in need of salvation. Looking in Scripture, we find it speaks of both. In Psalm 51, David gives us a view of being both loved and flawed:

> Have mercy on me, O God, according to your unfailing love; according to your great compassion blot out my transgressions. Wash away all my iniquity and cleanse me from my sin... Surely I was sinful at birth, sinful from the time my mother conceived me. Yet you desired faithfulness even in the womb; you taught me wisdom in that secret place. (Psalm 51:1–2, 5–6 NIV)

Part of our path of growth and healing was becoming less focused on performance and more focused on humbly living out of the identity and purpose God gave us as followers of Christ. These were our small movements of *being* instead of *doing*. When we integrated the good and the bad, little by little, we became less judgmental of each other. At the same time, as we marinated in how beloved we each were, we found more freedom to live and love out of our true identity. We won't experience perfect love and acceptance until heaven, but while we are here, with humility we can repair whenever we fall back into our old patterns. Larry Crabb describes in *Understanding Who You Are,*

> As creatures who bear God's image, we possess a unique dignity. It cannot be erased… The dignity of our individuality (the prints on my soul are as unique as those on my fingers) reflects God's creative genius. It reveals something of Him. It defines the self in each of us that, although defaced, can be restored and affirmed through an intimate relationship with Christ.[17]

Be a giver of love, not a receiver only

Let's be honest, we all want to be loved, and we are truly made for relationships. The bottom line Jesus spoke of in the Gospels was "love God and love others"—this is the greatest commandment. But this is impossible when I'm preoccupied with arranging my life, to make love and relationships work on my own terms. There is an ancient parable depicting the difference between heaven and hell. It describes the occupants of both places, sitting at long tables piled high with plates of delicious food. The people each have long spoons for arms that cannot bend. In hell, these long-armed inhabitants suffer and starve because they can't get the spoons in their mouths to feed themselves, and they refuse to feed each other. In heaven, the circumstances were exactly the same with long tables and amazing food, but these occupants scooped up the food and fed the person across the table from them. In this story, the setting for each group is the same, but the difference was in giving rather than getting.

When babies are born, they are precious little takers. Their whole survival depends on getting what they need from loving parents. Little by little, as they grow and develop, the demand to *get* is

---

[17] Larry Crabb, *Understanding Who You Are* (NavPress, 1997).

replaced with an understanding that the world doesn't revolve around them. Becoming a mature adult capable of having a healthy relationship depends on this *other* mindset. It's unfortunate, but many of us have arrested development and still operate as a child when it comes to love.

As we made this shift over many years of viewing ourselves by God's design as a mirror of his love and less about what we can get, we took responsibility for our actions and became less selfish. As a word of caution, though, we didn't change at exactly the same time or at the same rate. Neither did we simply make a pact to change, and everything was different. Growth occurs through all seasons. There were times when I was becoming more liberated, but Rob was stuck. There were also times when Rob was growing, but I was in a dry season. It's not always equal, but in the end, it takes two people willing to grow to make things better. This eventually led us to being more open, transparent, and honest with our flaws and the rough spots in our relationship. We share more on this in the chapter on intimacy.

What our triggers reveal

Most couples we've worked with have heard the term *trigger*, and when asked to define it, they usually think of it as any reaction, especially if it causes irritability or frustration. A trigger is a reaction, for sure, but it indicates something much deeper. Our triggers reveal the lies we believe about ourselves and others. For our purpose, we're defining a trigger as a reaction *not* commensurate with the situation or experience. It's an *overreaction*; the situation doesn't call for.

For example, there are certain things that annoy me, and for years, I just chalked it up to a preference. I really struggle with people who talk or scroll on their phones in movie theaters. My reaction was usually a quiet anger, irritation, and judgment of the insensitive troll who was doing it. Yes, it's annoying and distracting to have someone talk through a movie, but my reaction (although I felt justified at the time) was more intense than it should have been, revealing something deeper about me.

As I examined this, I realized my trigger was tied to my mother and how she behaved in my growing-up years. She was self-focused and rarely considered the impact she had on the people around her. She only thought of herself, her pain, and what she needed. As a result, I had deep-seated anger toward her for all the pain she caused me without ever owning it.

Although I knew in my head that God sees me and I matter to Him, I had a heightened sensitivity from the distorted view from my family that "I am invisible and unimportant," leading me to off-load those hurtful feelings in judgment. The situation in the movie theater and my experience with my mother are completely different, but my reaction to anyone who was self-absorbed was the same. When my feeling of *invisibility* was triggered, it interfered with my ability to respond appropriately instead of reacting. Once I understood this and processed the pain of that wound, I now had a choice in the movie theater or anywhere else. I could move away from that person, I could kindly ask them for what I wanted (which I couldn't do out of anger), or I could ignore their insensitive behavior.

When my kids were young, there were three things I strongly disciplined them for: lying, disrespect, and being critical of someone for something they couldn't change, like skin color, height, or family issues. All three things are good values to teach, but when I saw how my reactions were connected to my history and negative experiences with my parents, I could own my distorted views in those areas and lower my expectations and judgments.

Check engine light

Think of emotional triggers as a warning light, potentially from different types of hard or traumatic experiences. Rob and I were both triggered at times, but we didn't dig deep enough to find out the source of those triggers. Rob's reactions were more subtle than mine. He kept it inside. They were more like implosions, a silent form of judgment or passive aggression. Mine were often expressed verbally, or I would get quiet and pull away. Either way, our reactions were like the "Check Engine" light on the dashboard of our car, and for years, we ignored the light, hoping by some miracle the car would just keep running.

Most of us think of trauma as only harrowing large events, like physical, emotional, or sexual abuse; war; or natural disasters. These types of trauma are often referred to as "Large-T Trauma." These are painful, difficult, abusive, even dangerous experiences. There is another type of trauma called "small-t Trauma." These are the good and important things we needed but didn't receive. They often seem less dramatic but can be equally distressing, like emotional neglect or the general absence of care, nurturing, or security. Both types of trauma leave a mark on the heart that leads us to perpetually self-protect, but one is more obvious, and the other is more elusive and subtle.

If you were to ask us years ago about our childhoods, I would have said mine was messed up and traumatic, and Rob would have said his childhood was great, normal, even boring. What we discovered was we both experienced a form of trauma in our lives. Rob's trauma was "small t," while mine was more "Large T." This history showed up in our relationship in the ways we overreacted to situations and experiences and made it apparent we each had work to do. Even though the conclusions we formed were wrong, our different types of trauma were still driving the bus of our thoughts, beliefs, and behaviors, just in different ways.

Another consideration is that it's not a level playing field for those of us who have come from chaotic environments with physical, emotional, sexual abuse as well as violence and addictions. We often need more professional help because it is more than we can process on our own or in our small group at church. As much as I didn't like defining myself as abused or coming from what felt like a shameful family, facing reality and getting help to gradually be free from my history and the conclusions I formed were a critical step.

To better understand these triggers, let's look at the difference between responding and reacting. I encourage you to examine your own patterns. If you're like me, you'll discover you react more often than you thought. Then ask yourself the question, "Where is this reaction coming from?" If you stop blaming the situation or people around you, and if you're honest with yourself, you'll be surprised with your answers and the connections to your history.

Responding	*Reacting*
Responding is being able to distinguish thoughts and feelings.	*Reacting* lumps thoughts and emotions together.
Responding reflects or thinks before speaking.	*Reacting* says whatever in the heat of the moment.
Responding respects boundaries of others.	*Reacting* wants to control the lives of others.
Responding recognizes the existence of alternative views.	*Reacting* insists that all views be like its own.
Responding sees the context of another's behavior.	*Reacting* is quick to judge a person's character based on a single act.
Responding starts with asking questions in a nonthreatening way.	*Reacting* comes to quick conclusions without really knowing or asking.
Responding gives the benefit of the doubt first.	*Reacting* assumes the worst or the least about others.
Responding comes from a thoughtful mind in how it expresses emotions.	*Reacting* acts out on emotions without thinking.
Responding comes from internal decisions based on secure values.	*Reacting* results in external triggers from shaky and threatened beliefs.

For years, I made assumptions about myself and others without checking if they were valid or even true. I thought my reactions were justified, but what if they are telling me something, just like the Check Engine light in my car? What if I looked at my reactions as messengers, wanting to reveal to me an area where I need to be liberated? What if my simmering insecurities just under the surface are calling all the shots?

As we learned to recognize and pay attention to when we were triggered and explored the source of our reactions and responses more closely, Rob and I became safer with one another and discovered new depth and security in our relationship. This eventually led to greater trust, but as we will see in the next chapter, healing broken trust becomes a challenging and crucial layer in the journey of healing and recovery.

Discussion Questions

Chapter 4: Broken Self-Image

For personal reflection

1. Think about the connection between the comments your parents (or others) made about you and the way you thought of yourself growing up and now. Write your thoughts and some of the false beliefs you have.

2. How does the approval of others affect your life? Are you overly pleasing, in need of constant affirmation, or seeking something else from others?

3. Is there any part of Roxanne's letter to Rob you identify with? Which part and why?

4. If you didn't do this before, write out a description of how you view yourself without reference to your occupation, gender, children, or the things you do. Are you finding your worth by the response of others, or do you really believe your intrinsic value comes from God? What small steps would help you integrate His love for you? How well do you accept your strengths and weaknesses?

5. Read these verses and answer the questions:
   - John 15:15: "I do not call you servants anymore, because a servant doesn't know what his master is doing. I have called you friends, because I have made known to you everything I have heard from my Father." (I am *accepted* because _____?)
   - Philippians 4:12–13: "I know how to make do with little, and I know how to make do with a lot. In any and all circumstances I have learned the secret of being content—whether well fed or hungry, whether in abundance or in need. I am able to do all things through him who strengthens me." (I am *secure* because _____?)

- Ephesians 2:4–7: "But God, who is rich in mercy, because of his great love that he had for us, made us alive with Christ even though we were dead in trespasses. You are saved by grace! He also raised us up with him and seated us with him in the heavens in Christ Jesus, so that in the coming ages he might display the immeasurable riches of his grace through his kindness to us in Christ Jesus." (I am *significant* because _____?)

For group discussion

1. Rob struggled with the not-enough message and shame; what part of his thoughts do you identify with and why?

2. A trigger is an event or experience that sets off a memory tape or a flashback that ignites a reaction. It's usually an overreaction to a situation. It can be a sound, sight, touch, smell, etc. related to an earlier experience. When do you notice your overreactions, and how are they connected to your early history? What circumstances set you off? Share with your group some of your triggers; we all have them.

3. Review the chart on *Responding* versus *Reacting* and discuss small steps you can make in responding when a sensitive spot is triggered.

CHAPTER 5

Broken Trust

Fear is the path to the dark side. Fear leads to anger,
anger leads to hate, hate leads to suffering.

—Yoda

Roxanne

The foundation of any good relationship is trust, trust that the other person is being honest, that there are no secrets, trust that he or she will have your back and they are reliable. As well, we ideally need to *be* trusting, not overly suspicious or assuming the negative. Unfortunately, Rob and I both had issues in this area from our histories. I was not trusting because of what I saw, and Rob learned from his family to keep secrets—not a good combination.

I witnessed a mom lost in her alcoholism who never got the help she needed. Even though I have compassion for her being sick and the product of unresolved trauma from her childhood, it doesn't resolve my knee-jerk reaction to be less trusting. Up to her death at ninety-five, she still lied about even unimportant things. She kept secrets, manipulated, and found creative ways around the truth. She came to know Jesus in her fifties, which I believe gave her a level of comfort, but despite what she learned about living the Christian life, she still struggled to keep her darker side in check. She never took the time or effort to learn why she drank or why she was a hoarder. She didn't (or wouldn't) do the work to explore the impact of her history or allow God to liberate her from her self-imposed prison.

When we marry, we don't just marry the person, we also marry the whole family. It's not Rob's fault I was raised to be suspicious, and he's been on the receiving end of my suspicions many times. I was trained to sniff out, look for, and be suspicious when things didn't add up. This created a perfect storm for us because Rob learned as a child to keep secrets and see what he could get away with, which, as it turns out, was quite a bit. There were many things I didn't know when we first got married, and some of the stories of his past weren't revealed until our marriage had almost crumbled. I had a gut feeling something didn't add up, but I didn't have concrete reasons not to trust him. My ability to trust was already weak, so I questioned my own ability to judge the situation correctly and usually assumed it was my issue.

My lack of trust was not limited to people; I struggled with God as well. I began a relationship with Jesus Christ in college, and I longed to trust God more easily, but lingering doubts still persisted. Could God really be trusted? If so, why do terrible things happen to good people? I had an *equational* mindset. My formula was: follow the rules + God is pleased = good results (in marriage, raising kids, life in general). But this formula didn't play out as I had hoped.

This black-and-white way of thinking might seem comforting when you're trying to control outcomes, but is it really? Since my trust button was broken, I became overly self-protective. I doubted God, and when it was difficult for me to trust an all-powerful God, I assumed I must be the problem. I became quietly controlling to protect myself from pain.

As much as we hate to admit it, everyone is controlling in some way. Control is part of our fallen nature, and it's often expressed in lack of trust. At times trust felt foolish to me, like the old expression, "Fool me once, shame on you. Fool me twice, shame on me." Just in case you don't think you have these tendencies, here is a list of the most common forms of control, which show up as defensiveness, and I was guilty of most.

Common Forms of Defensiveness

Perfectionism	Trying to fix others	Being defensive
Being the victim	Using anger or guilt to intimidate	Telling people what to do
Pleasing others	Bragging	Withholding information

Rob

Fire can warm or consume, water can quench or drown, wind can caress or cut. And so it is with human relationships: we can both create and destroy, nurture and terrorize, traumatize and heal each other.[18]

Healing broken trust

Trust has different meanings to different people. To some, it might mean feeling safe with your partner, knowing they will respect your physical and emotional boundaries, knowing your partner listens when you express needs and feelings. To others, it may mean not hiding things from your partner, respecting each other, being vulnerable with each other, supporting each other. Like a multifaceted diamond, I think it includes all of the above.

Trust is an essential component of a strong relationship, but it doesn't happen quickly. Once broken, trust can be hard to rebuild, but it is possible.

Because I grew up in a family where I felt invisible and on my own, my childhood was obviously different from Roxanne's, but

---

[18] Bruce D. Perry and M. Szalavitz, *The Boy Who Was Raised As a Dog: And Other Stories from a Child Psychiatrist's Notebook: What Traumatized Children Can Teach Us About Loss, Love, and Healing* (Basic Books, 2017).

like her, my ability to trust was broken as well. Significant people in my life became unreliable and unpredictable. With inconsistent and unavailable connections at home, those who should have been there to pay attention to my emotional needs weren't available. That eventually led me to not trusting anyone would be there for me if I needed them, anyway.

During these early years, I learned to hide what I was doing, lie about where I was going, or who I was with, and I could get away with just about anything. As a result, I learned the opposite of trust; I learned how to be untrustworthy. I learned how to be secretive. I learned how to be deceptive.

It wasn't until years later in our marriage while sitting in a counselor's office that I began to recognize how my secrecy, deception, dishonesty, rationalizing, and breaking promises were exactly what Roxanne experienced with her mother. Her mother was dishonest, secretive, and unreliable, and when I behaved in a similar way, it touched the pain of her childhood wounds. It broke my heart as I began to understand the impact this had on her, but at another level, I was also recognizing the impact of my own history on me. Often, we are so wrapped up in our own struggles, we fail to see how they are impacting and hurting those we love the most.

Healing sexual brokenness

"Sexual brokenness" has become a frequently used term, and in my life it described the break in trust and emotional separation in our marriage. But what does this term really mean? When we speak of relational and sexual brokenness, we are talking about the struggles and temptations women and men fight against while they live on this earth and the negative impact this struggle has on their lives.

No matter how hard I tried or how many promises I made to myself and others, my ability to make my life work was getting worse instead of getting better. By becoming emotionally and relationally separated from Roxanne, I became more separated from myself as well, unable to identify or adequately express feelings or emotions.

Sadly, I also become separated from God, unable to connect with him in a meaningful way. At this stage, nothing in life worked the way I thought it should work, and our relationship became a prime target for trying to get from each other what is only available from God. Our broken trust cut deeply. But the hope of healing, restoration, and forgiveness broke into our brokenness by God's grace.

Jay Stringer writes about what's at the heart or the core of sexual brokenness. He says, "The root problems driving sexual brokenness are broken family systems, abuse, trauma, and a lack of purpose."[19] My story clearly involves all four. Many individuals struggling with sexual brokenness come from families characterized as either rigid or disengaged. A rigid family typically uses power to manipulate and control behavior, while a disengaged family abdicates power at the time when a child needs guidance the most. My family was disengaged, and never knowing who had the power, I resorted to behaviors that gave me at least some sense of power and control. To survive in a family system such as this, children often learn to become fairly resilient, which I was. But without performing in a way to earn and secure love, I didn't believe I had any value to others or possibly wasn't loved at all.

Consider what it was like for your partner growing up in his family. Was it a rigid or disengaged family system? What was modeled to him regarding trust growing up? Remember, most of what men learned about masculinity, marriage, sex, and intimacy was *caught* rather than *taught*. I grew up in the "Marlboro Man" generation, a rugged cowboy on horseback with a cigarette in his mouth. Today, just look at men's cologne ads or a host of other images for clothing, cars, sportswear, etc. Apart from being taught what true masculinity looks like by wise mentors, boys grow up with distorted role models and come to distorted conclusions.

Disengaged families release children into the world with a host of unmet needs. Men who were raised in these families often compromise integrity to seek out fleeting experiences of intimacy.

---

[19] Stringer.

In contrast, rigid family structures have rules that are never to be questioned, and there can be elements of fear and control. Seeds of anger grow out of rigid family systems, and seeds of lust thrive in disengaged families.

As a young boy in my disengaged family, my attraction to unhealthy sexual behavior was an attempt to escape feeling unwanted and to deal with feeling invisible. Years later, as an adult, I found myself repeating a cycle of shame, regret, and guilt, unable to manage stress in healthy ways. I learned that trust and intimacy were not to be found in the family I grew up in but outside of it, and I packed that broken belief in my trailer, hooked it to my bumper, and towed it into my marriage. I had a lot to learn about trust—about broken trust—and about being trustworthy.

Roxanne

Fearing I had a greater-than-average chance of marrying an alcoholic, I was reluctant to get married, but Rob was so steady, I felt confident I had dodged that bullet. Maybe it was my naivete, but it never occurred to me I could marry some other type of addiction or *-ism*. At the twenty-five-year mark into our marriage, my suspicions about Rob's sexual integrity began to surface. I didn't think he was having an affair, but I wondered about his lack of interest in sex compared to the early years.

Some women in my Bible study groups complained about how often their husbands asked for sex, and I remained uncomfortably silent on the issue. Despite the divide in our relationship and our attempts at repair, I still tried to be available to him and felt guilty about long periods of time without connecting intimately. But he seemed so indifferent. One afternoon, as we strolled around a lake near our home, I asked why he wasn't interested in me. I wondered if he secretly resented how I spent my money. He assured me the answer was no. I asked if it was difficult for him when he traveled to avoid the temptation of adult entertainment on hotel TVs, and again, he said, "No, I'm always too tired or working."

I asked, "Then help me understand the issue."

These conversations felt like a poker game. He was careful not to show his cards and would give me one card at a time. I never knew what cards he was holding. In the absence of information, most people fill in the blanks with not-so-positive scenarios, which I did. Even though I raised two sons, I left the "guy talk" conversations to Rob.

What I didn't know was Rob was not altogether whole in this area, so how could he honestly guide them? I was hoping I was wrong and my gut impressions were just my insecurities. I hate to be unfairly judged myself, so I wanted more evidence before I would let my mind go there.

My suspicions came to a head when Rob shared something he was learning about his tendencies toward addictive behavior from a book he was reading. He never mentioned anything about pornography; it was more about his history with drugs, alcohol, and dating in college. He talked about getting in touch with the unhealthy ways he handled stress and anxiety. I thought most of those struggles were in the past, occurring way before he became a Christian and long before we were married. I thought I knew about his past, but I didn't know he had never really worked through his broken views of sexuality. We never talked about it as a couple. This was one of the weaknesses in our marriage.

I continued to worry about what was going on in our relationship. One day, I was doing some online shopping and came across some suspicious Internet search history. When I confronted him with what I saw, he confessed and acknowledged visiting inappropriate sites. He was tired of hiding and covering up something he knew was eating him alive. I understood the temptation, especially since we were struggling in our relationship, and pornography is so easily accessible, but more difficult and damaging were the years of dishonesty and deceit, especially when I had asked about it directly. This was an especially hard blow to my already-damaged trust button.

The shame of confession and revealing a secret struggle was too much for him. Despite Rob's love for me and our relationship, the strong pull to avoid shame and embarrassment along with the desire to be respected and seen in a positive light was keeping him stuck in the cycle of secrecy. These competing and conflicting desires, along with the effort it takes to protect a false image were exhausting for him.

Some wives put pornography in the same category as an affair, and there is an argument to be made for considering it a form of unfaithfulness. As we've worked with couples experiencing this issue, it tends to go in two general directions. One response is total blame without trying to understand what's beneath the behavior, the other is ignoring, minimizing, and excusing the behavior. Neither way of coping is truthful or helpful. Here are some common myths or statements women tell themselves about this intruder in their relationship.

1. If I lose weight or become more attractive, he won't look at porn.
2. If we have sex more often, that is the answer.
3. Somehow, it's my fault.
4. Everyone uses porn; I need to accept that it's expected and normal.
5. Porn usage doesn't affect our relationship.

These are some of the lies, questions, and thoughts that go through our minds as we try to make sense of unhealthy behaviors that damage relationships. It feels uncomfortably powerless when we can't control or change the habits or choices of another person, especially when they so painfully impact our lives. Although a wife can have an influence, only he can choose to surrender to God, control his sexual appetites, renew his mind and habits, and get in touch with what lies beneath counterfeit ways of coping and his distorted understanding of intimacy. This goes way beyond self-control to a deeper understanding of the lies he believes and turning from them to a loving and forgiving God.

It's important to recognize that pornography and other types of compromised sexual integrity are symptoms of something deeper. I'm not excusing this break in trust, and neither did Rob once he stopped rationalizing and minimizing the impact. I wished he had been courageous enough to talk with me about it earlier. I also wish both of us had a better understanding of what's beneath this unwanted behavior. Even though I heard it was every man's battle, I was ignorant of how universal and widespread this problem is.

Rob knew pornography was poisoning our marriage, breaking down trust, and hurting himself, but he was caught in a destructive cycle of deceit and shame. I was hurt, but I also knew in my heart, I wasn't much better than him. Although I was never attracted to pornography, when I felt lonely and forgotten, I remember thinking if some guy came along who was kind, expressed interest in me, and temporarily relieved my pain, I might have fallen too. We both had work to do to rebuild our broken trust, not just from what happened between us but also from our early family histories.

Rob: It's Time to Wake Up!

You may be familiar with the account in the Bible of what happened to the prophet Jonah who ran from God when he was told to go preach to the city of Nineveh. This was one of the largest cities in the known world and also a city known for unbelievable evil and cruelty. In Jonah's mind, these people didn't deserve God, so instead, he got on a boat headed for the city of Tarshish, which was three thousand miles in the opposite direction. To cut to the chase, God interrupted Jonah's journey when he was thrown overboard and swallowed by "a great fish."

Rather than offering theological commentary on whether the account of Jonah and the gigantic fish is a true historical account or an allegory, I prefer to share how God used Jonah's experience in my life. For nearly twenty years, I was running, like Jonah. I thought I was running to something new, something more meaningful and important. In reality, I was running away from something. Dragging my family with me wherever the journey led, we moved four times, and I had six different jobs, all in less than ten years. In my workaholic panic, as I ran for my version of Tarshish. I focused on the next opportunity, bigger job, more success, more money, more influence. Work truly became my mistress. But alongside the work mistress, I was still struggling with how I coped with stress and anxiety through inappropriate and unwanted sexual behavior.

In Jonah's story, he was asleep in the bottom of the boat when a storm hit. In much the same way, I had fallen asleep. I had fallen asleep and found myself in a storm where I tried to convince myself that chasing the next opportunity, running after bigger and better challenges would bring satisfaction. All the while, I continued unhealthy and unwanted sexual behavior as an acceptable way of relieving my stress. I rationalized, I justified, I made excuses, but in my heart, I felt guilty, cloaked in shame, and weighed down by the secrecy and deception I was carrying. I repeatedly told myself, "I'm not this man." I would pray, make promises to change, read the Bible, rationalize my behavior, and keep it hidden. Apart from learning how to deal with stress in my life in healthier ways, I continually returned to old behaviors, and the painful cycle of failure continued.

We were in a beautiful setting in Colorado Springs when I had another conversation with my friend Larry Crabb. In his gracious and compassionate way, he introduced me to what he called my "core terror." He asked, "What do you think is at the very core of your being that you're afraid of and will do almost anything to protect from being exposed?" I made some feeble attempts to say something that sounded insightful, but Larry interrupted me and said, "Rob, your core terror is weightlessness." He said it was fear of not measuring up to others, not being enough, not mattering. I was not surprised to hear this, but I was surprised that someone else could see it. I thought I did a pretty good job of keeping what was beneath the surface hidden from others.

Larry encouraged me to examine this core terror of *weightlessness* and how it may be at the root of my anxious pursuit of influence, being noticed, being connected with the right people, having financial security. But there was a root beneath all this that he was inviting me to examine. At the heart of my core fear was a belief that I needed to prove my worth to earn love but that I would never achieve it and would be left behind.

Roxanne shared the illustration in her journal of feeling like she had fallen in the water while water skiing. Unaware she was no longer behind or even in the boat and was treading water in the lake, I drove on. I remember how painful it felt when she read that journal entry to me for the first time. For nearly twenty years, I had left her in the water on her own to stay afloat. I made excuses for why I wasn't present and attentive. I was selfishly taking care of myself, and although I didn't come out and say it exactly this way, I was saying, "I'll take care of me. You take care of you."

Reading her story, I wept at the picture she painted of how she felt. She was now experiencing abandonment from me like she did with her mother, and I was moving more into isolation and independence I learned in my family. We were both retreating into old patterns and moving further away from each other.

During that last conversation, Larry gently put his hand on my shoulder, and although it sounds harsh, it was delivered with compassion. He said, "If hell is 'aloneness,' you have created a chaotic condition for Roxanne that is as near to hell as it could be." Was I like Jonah who fell asleep? Had I become numb to what was going on around me?

Now, if you find yourself reacting strongly to this, let me assure you that he did not say this to be cruel. Larry was a kind and trusted mentor and had earned the right to be honest with me. He was never cruel or insensitive, but he was lovingly honest and direct. I can only pray that the men in your life have someone in their lives who has permission to be just as caring, just as loving, and just as honest. Through my trusted friend Larry Crabb, God was saying to me, "Wake up, Rob!"

Who's whispering "wake up" in the ear of the men in your life?

We were rapidly becoming a marriage on life support. Looking back, I don't blame her, but as she shares it, Roxanne was losing trust and respect to the point that it had become *contempt*. What does it mean to have contempt for someone? Coming from the root word for *scorn* or *disdain*, contempt means you despise or strongly disapprove—difficult words to swallow. The question in my mind became, "Can I win someone back who has contempt for me?"

Roxanne: Rebuilding Trust... There Is Hope

If you are struggling with this same issue in your marriage, I'm so sorry. I wish I could look you in the eye and assure you of God's love and concern for you both. If you have read this far, I'm going to assume you want more than just pain relief. You may be wondering why I waited until halfway through this book to address this all-too-common problem of broken trust. But to be able to work through our pain, we first needed to lay the foundation of awareness, new skills, and new habits. We needed to face our broken thinking and damaged self-images so we could talk about, as well as have compassion for how our histories affected us.

Our past is not an excuse, but it offers an explanation

Because of my black-and-white thinking, I was prone to judgment and concluded, "What Rob did was wrong, and there are no excuses, so peace out." This made it extremely hard and unsafe for anyone to be honest with me. However, as I learned to see our marriage from God's perspective—that although we were flawed, we were loved—I took responsibility for my issues. This helped free Rob to own his issues, choices, and behavior without the fear of constant condemnation. Would there be questions? Yes. Did we need to give and receive forgiveness? Eventually, yes. Accountability? Of course. But condemnation and judgment? No! Remember, in Christ, there is no condemnation.

> Therefore there is now no condemnation at
> all for those who are in Christ Jesus. (Romans
> 8:1 CSB)

Our purpose for writing this book is primarily to offer hope. In our marriage, the odds were stacked against us. Both my parents had been married four times, we lived years doing things the wrong way, we each had issues from our past hindering our ability to trust God and love well, and we both had various forms of sin we knew were damaging. But God is faithful and doesn't give up on us. Maybe because we're from the boomer generation we hung in there all these years, not wanting to be another statistic. But I think in our heart of hearts, we had hope (maybe just a tiny flicker at times) that God would liberate us from the individual bondage of our past, and in a weird way, He used our imperfections and brokenness to do it.

I'm sure the healing journey would have been even harder and taken much longer if Rob actually had an affair. If you are in that situation, we know it's like a bomb going off in your relationship. It's devastating, and we have seen and felt that pain walking alongside our own family members and friends. In some cases, despite their injuries, many are able to repair and forge a much healthier relationship, while others don't get past the hurt and end up divorced. But the single most significant difference between those who repair and those who don't is not only when the offender takes responsibility for the pain and suffering they caused but also when both are able to understand how their histories contributed to the breakdown.

Talk is cheap. Regret and promises alone are not enough. When trust has been broken in a relationship, when there are secrets, when hiding and rationalizing behavior has entered, shame, regret, and fear have also taken up residence. Again, the process of restoration takes time, courage, and persistence.

As we stepped into our healing journey, accountability and changes in behavior followed. We started learning to change our thoughts, beliefs, and habits. There is hope because God loves you, and He is for you. Navigating these troubled waters requires both of you to be willing to ask for help and humbly work toward reconciliation. Healing broken trust due to infidelity is a big topic, and many excellent books have been devoted solely to this subject. In the appendix, we offer a list of suggested resources and practical tools we found helpful.

Our real enemy

Another factor we underestimated was the enemy of our souls, who wants our marriage to fail. We spent so much time blaming each other, we lost sight of our common enemy, who will do his best to derail and neutralize us from being vessels of God's love. This is not to simply shrug our shoulders and say, "The devil made me do it," or make the mistake of overestimating his power or underestimating his influence but to acknowledge there is a battle and we have a real enemy.

When we first got married, I think we envisioned being on *The Love Boat*. There might be some rough waters from time to time, but God had us in the palm of His hand. We soon discovered, however, we were on an aircraft carrier heading toward the Persian Gulf. Yes, God's love and protection were available to us, but we weren't asking. Again, our pattern wasn't outwardly dramatic with bombs going off overhead, but the war was still raging. I don't think even our closest friends knew how badly we were doing. We were really good at faking it. My *go-to* behavior was to become numb and nice, which is exactly what I did to survive the war in my home growing up.

As I became aware of how the enemy worked to tear each of us down, I could see he did it in totally different ways. His biggest tool against me was discouragement and wallowing in self-pity. Working together, those two thoughts quickly took me down a rabbit hole, leaving me hopeless. Once I realized this tactic, I was on alert for those subtle temptations. I discovered warning statements or words he whispered in my ear like, "You poor thing. This is hopeless. People don't change," and "Why bother?"

Some of Rob's tempting thoughts were, "You're on your own. You don't have what it takes. You'll never measure up," and "You're such a disappointment." These whispered lies needed to be recognized, refuted, and replaced with truth. Rob's unhealthy ways of coping with these lies were to distract himself by marathon running, working endless hours, and finishing a master's degree in psychology no less. His avoidance of intimacy with me led to counterfeit nonrelational substitutes. His path toward healing involved learning how to talk about what he felt and taking action steps for accountability and honesty with me and other trusted men.

Instead of just wailing and complaining in my journals, I began to pray more specifically for Rob and myself. I spent more time thanking God for His character than asking for a lengthy list of wants only to relieve my pain. Rob and I agreed that in our relationship no topic was off-limits. He discovered he didn't have a vocabulary for feeling words and worked hard not only to expand the ability to describe his emotional state but also how to be more present in conversations and talk about those feelings.

We agreed to be completely honest with each other. Realizing and accepting that my partner is not the enemy was a significant part of our journey. There's something bonding and connecting about forming an alliance against a common enemy.

There will be no secrets

There is power in community. Rob got involved with other men with similar stories, giving him the courage to be honest and talk about his struggle. He was understanding how impossible it is to solve this issue alone. He was learning to recognize and fight temptations he'd given into for years and surrender to God's sustaining grace to make new habits of the heart. As he took these steps to be more open and honest, the poker games and vague answers became less and less.

This was not an overnight process, but as I gained confidence in his sincere efforts, my trust and respect began to grow. These steps became the drops in the bucket that helped rebuild trust. Once the truth came to light, we made a commitment to keep no secrets even for small seemingly insignificant things. This was pivotal for both of us to heal.

Tackling your fears

Helen Keller said, "Life is a bold adventure, or it is nothing at all."[20] Unlike me, Helen Keller conquered fears I can only imagine. Fear was my constant companion since childhood, and I was more

---

[20] Helen Keller, *Let Us Have Faith* (Doubleday, 1940).

preoccupied looking for safety than living boldly. My biggest fear was rejection and abandonment. My fear of being left alone started in a hospital at fifteen months old and continued throughout childhood.

Years later after having three children, I remember fearing Rob's dying when he went away on long ministry trips. In the early 1980s, he went to China for six weeks. We didn't have cell phones in those days, so I was on my own for that length of time. I allowed the fears to run rampant, picturing my life without him, planning the funeral and all. It seems silly now, but my early experiences trained me to think of the worst to somehow prepare myself for it.

What was the real issue? What was the source of all that fear? I didn't believe I had what it takes to make it alone and handle the pain, and I wasn't entirely sure God was enough either. Unlike Helen Keller, I was lacking courage and faith. I don't say this to shame myself but to be honest with where I needed to grow.

Recently, I was with a group of women at a baby shower, and the topic of childbirth inevitably (and sometimes insensitively) came up. There's sort of a fellowship of suffering in telling our birth stories and how we lived to tell the gnarly details. Despite all the classes to normalize the experience and all the tips on breathing and relaxation, I still doubted I could do it, especially before my first baby. True to form, our first child's birth took many, many hours, and when I reached the point of exhaustion, I declared I was done (as if). Everyone else in the room knew I couldn't just quit, and they were confident I had what it took to get her out, but at the time, the pain was too much, and no amount of prayer, breathing, ice chips, or hand-holding relieved it.

The next child followed only fourteen months later, and again I feared a difficult delivery. This time, I knew what to expect, making it worse. But God, in His grace, allowed this baby to pop out with little effort or pain. By the third child, I still wasn't looking forward to the process, but I knew I could get through it, and I did, although still not easy.

Do you see the progression? Each time I made it through, my confidence grew in God and myself. In each experience, I doubted but still pushed through; I couldn't quit. To get to the other side, I faced the pain and worked with it rather than pushing against it, and I had loving people encouraging me to press on. That's why most women compare any potential physical pain to childbirth. "This root canal is no fun, but it's easier than giving birth."

In so many of the challenges I have faced in my marriage or personal health issues, the concept is the same. Depending on how bad the circumstances are, I often reach a point of desperation and doubt if I can make it or if God will help me. But He brings me through even if a bit bruised.

I had a false definition of love. As a child, I felt loved when my father would rescue me from my mother when she was drunk, relieving my pain and fear. This six-year-old belief system was what I thought God should do if he loved me. If God did not quickly fix my situation, He must not love me. I couldn't see it at the time, but He was working *in me*, which was much more liberating than just relieving my pain.

Just like childbirth, the pain and the process have a purpose. Looking back at trials I've gone through, I see his love and transforming power, freeing me bit by bit from the stranglehold of fear.

The common acrostic for fear is *False Evidence Appearing Real.* There is nothing false about physical or relational pain. What is false are the lies and wrong conclusions I choose to believe, like God is not faithful to carry me, help me, or sustain me. What is false is believing I can predict the future, instead of living in the moment and trusting God with my future.

For me, the path out of living in fear was gradual and not overnight. It was a process of seeing God differently as my constant and caring friend, sympathetic to my weakness and trials, and not a far-off all-powerful deity who wasn't concerned or compassionate.

Wherever you are in your pain, you have a choice. I've often heard Kay Yerkovich say in her How We Love seminars, "It's painful to stay where you are and not grow, and it's painful to change. Staying where you are will keep you stuck, but making the decision to change will liberate you, so pick your pain." It was painful to face my fears but equally painful (or perhaps more so) not to. When I realized my fears were controlling my life in a harmful way, I became determined to tackle my *false* conclusions, and live in the reality of *truth*.

Finding forgiveness

I wrestle with forgiveness, partly because of what I saw growing up and partly the human part of me that wants justice more than grace. I saw forgiveness as letting someone off the hook or giving them a hall pass, even though I know Christ has sacrificially forgiven me. My human side wants to balance the scales. Maybe I've been too influenced by our American sense of justice more than by God's way of grace, reconciliation, and forgiveness.

In the years I was harboring unforgiveness, I was not only harming the relationship but also in large part, I was harming myself. My hurt led me to feel contempt for Rob, and that is a toxic emotion. I suspect many of my physical health problems became way worse during this time. In my forties, during a particularly stressful time in our marriage, I developed a seizure disorder. It may have been coincidental or genetic, or maybe I was poisoning myself with contempt.

Marriage researchers have identified contempt as the most dangerous and toxic emotion and a major predictor of couples who divorce. Some of us need to forgive ourselves, our parents, siblings, or an abuser, and the lack of forgiveness becomes toxic in more ways than we can imagine. God commands us to be like Him, and He is forgiving. God created us and knows exactly what we need physically, emotionally, spiritually, relationally. There is peace in being transformed into His image, even though the process is hard at times and feels confusing when He uses pain to bring release. Forgiveness brings release.

The Greek word for forgive is *aphiemi*, which means, "to send away." This passage is asking us to "send away" the sin committed against us. But this is challenging when there have been years of offense, and we've been deeply wounded. So how can we get our arms around what it really means to forgive? It *does not* mean forgetting; that's impossible. It *does not* mean you never get angry or sad about the state of your marriage now or in the future. It also *does not* mean you can't talk about ways you've hurt each other or have clear boundaries. What it *does* mean is you are not going to hold these things over your spouse's head any longer or make the other person *pay* for something indefinitely. Forgiveness also means you are willing to "own up" to how you contributed to the marital distress that led to problems in the first place because no partner is 100 percent innocent.

Forgiveness is a decision

Forgiveness is a process often beginning with a decision to forgive, even if the emotions aren't there yet. It's an attitude of the heart that needs to become a lifestyle even in the unfortunate event of separation or divorce. No matter what happens to the marriage, God is doing something within you. What if you grow in grace and forgiveness so that the rest of your lives are healthier and at peace? Often, couples are not healthy enough to divorce because they have unfinished business, and they inflict that pain, suffering, and unforgiveness on their kids or into their next relationships.

I knew I needed to forgive my mom. I needed to forgive Rob. Forgiveness was the right thing to do, but my feelings didn't always cooperate. It's healthy to acknowledge and explore feelings, but my decisions still need to be based on values, goals, and the invitation of God. But if I waited for my feelings to fall in line before following God in life's challenging decisions, I would never have written this book. Neither would I exercise or eat right or play Legos with my kids or a hundred other things.

To put it simply, forgiveness is a gift you give yourself. It can free you from bitterness and hurt if you are holding on to your right for justice. On the other hand, trust is not the same as forgiveness. Trust is earned, and broken trust is built and restored over time with consistent action.

Forgiveness takes courage. Depending on your ability to truly hear one another, you might need help in this important area. Old habits of communication die hard, and the hurt and pain can be intense. You may need to get help from a wise coach or counselor, and we will offer some suggestions on this in the last chapter.

Discussion Questions

Chapter 5: Broken Trust

For personal reflection

1. Describe how you identify with Roxanne's broken trust and the ways you tend to control.
2. Before your husband's or partner's issues began being revealed, did you have difficulty trusting (like Roxanne), or were you too trusting? What do you think that's tied to?
3. What parts of Rob's thoughts helped you see inside a man's brain or thinking process?
4. On a one-to-ten scale, how fearful are you? The more controlling, the more fearful. Do you believe God is not going to care for you so you need to overly protect yourself?

For group discussion

1. As you heal personally or as a couple, how does the enemy try to trip you up? What thoughts or situations does he used to take you down? These could be things like the children acting up, illness, work-related stress, or things breaking down like the car. What can you do to recognize and resist the enemy's influence over you?
2. How has the fear of change, abandonment, or judgment caused you to stay stuck? Do you identify with thinking you can't go on, like wanting to quit in the midst of labor while giving birth? Write out your thoughts on this and share with a trusted friend or group.
3. What is your understanding of forgiveness, and where did that come from? Are you waiting for feelings before forgiving? What's the difference between forgiveness and reconciliation?

4. Read Matthew 18:21–35. What is God inviting you to regarding forgiveness?

Then Peter approached him and asked, "Lord, how many times must I forgive my brother or sister who sins against me? As many as seven times?"

"I tell you, not as many as seven," Jesus replied, "but seventy times seven.

"For this reason, the kingdom of heaven can be compared to a king who wanted to settle accounts with his servants. When he began to settle accounts, one who owed ten thousand talents was brought before him. Since he did not have the money to pay it back, his master commanded that he, his wife, his children, and everything he had be sold to pay the debt.

"At this, the servant fell facedown before him and said, 'Be patient with me, and I will pay you everything.' Then the master of that servant had compassion, released him, and forgave him the loan.

"That servant went out and found one of his fellow servants who owed him a hundred denarii. He grabbed him, started choking him, and said, 'Pay what you owe!'

"At this, his fellow servant fell down and began begging him, 'Be patient with me, and I will pay you back.' But he wasn't willing. Instead, he went and threw him into prison until he could pay what was owed. When the other servants saw what had taken place, they were deeply distressed and went and reported to their master everything that had happened. Then, after he had summoned him, his master said to him, 'You wicked servant! I forgave you all that debt because you begged me. Shouldn't you also have had mercy on your fellow servant, as I had mercy on you?' And because he was angry, his master handed him over to the jailers to be tortured until he could pay everything that was owed. So also my heavenly Father will do to you unless every one of you forgives his brother or sister from your heart." (Matthew 18:21–35 CSB)

CHAPTER 6

Broken Intimacy

Roxanne

This is the hardest chapter for me to write, especially for someone who experienced such brokenness in this area. The term intimacy is often grossly misunderstood, making it even harder for me to define. It's often referred to as *Into*-Me-*See*, being willing and open to see and to be seen, and this kind of *knowing* takes time to develop. It's the culmination of friendship, safety, acceptance, which then, in a committed relationship, can lead to physical intimacy. No one from my early history really knew and accepted me with all my flaws. I was hoping marriage would be the answer, and Rob certainly knows me better than anyone else in this world, but it also came with almost equal amounts of hurt and rejection.

In our culture today, we see both men and women are confused in this area. In our highly sexualized culture, people look to each other as the primary source of being known and loved and narrowly define intimacy as sex alone. Physical intimacy with another human being is designed by God to be the expression or result of a relationship where two souls meet, commit, and connect emotionally and spiritually at the deepest possible levels.

> Sex is like fire. It's beautiful and warming
> in the right setting or conditions but deadly and

destructive without healthy limits, boundaries, and understanding.

Most women I speak with want closeness, affection, and safety before sex. It's not that women don't have casual sex (especially for the 30 percent of us who have been abused in this area) it's just not satisfying, meaningful, or even safe without the emotional component. Because of our misunderstandings in this area, many are much more open to being naked physically while keeping their souls fully clothed and hidden. It's not too far off to say most of us are woefully ignorant of God's design for intimacy emotionally, spiritually, and physically. We hide from real love and authenticity mostly because it reveals our fear and vulnerability to being hurt, but we don't express this fear in the same way.

I thought I was an open and honest person, but there were parts of me (especially when we grew apart) I kept hidden from Rob, almost unconsciously. In the book of Genesis, when Adam and Eve sinned, they hid from God and from each other. That's when shame entered the equation. I had a fear of intimacy from my history that went beyond sex. Here is a list of some of the signs of fear, which could be true for women or men:

Fear of Intimacy Symptoms

Low self-esteem	Trouble forming or committing to close relationships
Trust issues	A history of unstable relationships
Being superficial	Difficulty sharing feelings
Experience episodes of anger	Actively avoid physical contact
Difficulty expressing emotion	Insatiable sexual desire

Roxanne's history of intimacy

My introduction to sexuality and false intimacy happened when I was just six years old. A boy around twelve years old asked me to play a game with him which then became his way of exploring his own blossoming hormones. I didn't like or understand this game; it almost felt like I was a substitute for a blow-up doll he could practice on. It was weird and uncomfortable but fortunately didn't go too far when my father caught him in the act. The boy was disciplined severely, and I feared the same would happen to me.

Despite all the chaos of our lives at that time, my father handled it compassionately. He assured me it wasn't my fault and what the boy did was wrong and to never let him touch me that way again. I was relieved I wasn't in trouble but still felt a bit of shame and confusion. When sex is introduced to a young child in any form, it causes a crack in their emotional foundation and awakens something that should be fast asleep for years to come.

Fast-forward to my teen years, I still never had a helpful or clear conversation about sex with anyone, except my girlfriends. We just pooled our ignorance, and all we heard was guys wanted it (a lot) and you could get pregnant.

I didn't become a Christian until I was nineteen, and the '60s and '70s were a time of "free love," drugs, and rock and roll. To avoid following in my mother's footsteps, I did not drink or party wildly. I saw what loss of control did to her. Since fear was always rumbling under the surface, I also avoided "going all the way" sexually, fearing I might get pregnant. In my mind, I was sure my father would disown me if I came home with that news. It's not that I wasn't tempted, but fear, doom, and predicting the worst case kept me in line rather than any type of moral compass.

By my junior year of high school, I'd found my voice in many ways and felt reasonably good about how I looked, although I still struggled with my Armenian nose and curly hair. I went to great lengths to straighten it by sleeping on giant rollers and taping my bangs down (no blow-dryers or flat irons in those days). Long straight hair was the style, and fitting in was more important than being yourself or different. My much-older stepsister used to say I was beautifully exotic. Not what I wanted to hear because the girls on the front of *Teen* magazine were blond, blue-eyed, small-nosed Barbie dolls. This goes beyond being stylish but to questioning my worth by how I look. Despite my popularity, I think I was still struggling with my brother's nickname label *Ugh*.

I threw myself into school clubs, cheerleading, art classes, guitar lessons, and dance. I enjoyed all the arts and the sense of belonging that came with these social events. I liked the vote of confidence of being pursued, being liked, and feeling attractive. Maybe I wasn't so ugly after all. I had many boyfriends during high school and college and experimented with affection and "making out," always thinking about where the limits were. Some of these relationships were fun and romantic, going to concerts and out for dinner.

In my sophomore year before I could drive, one friend, who was particularly nice, consistently found me as I walked to school and gave me a ride in his *souped-up* Trans Am. I knew most guys were out for just one thing, but I also formed an immature and idealistic belief that if someone really likes or loves you, he will pursue you, anticipate your needs, and treat you special with pure and selfless motives. This later became an issue in our marriage because Rob had never been treated this way and had no clue how to offer it to me. I had my own broken and confused understanding of love and intimacy, and he had his.

When it came to sex, many of the Christian guys I dated were not much different than the non-Christians even though I was able to stave them off. In my friendliness, they must have interpreted that to mean I was asking, which I wasn't. I concluded all men had sex on the brain no matter how much they claimed to love Jesus. Their hormones and lightning-fast reactions to any visual stimuli are beyond my comprehension and a reality I grossly underestimated. So I thought it unlikely I would find anyone who could be trusted with my heart; I was friendly but kept an arm's length.

In high school and well into our marriage, it never crossed my mind men were so influenced by pornography. Porn was not as available as it is now, but where there's a will, there's a way. When I met

Rob, he wasn't like the other guys I dated. He took things slower and never pushed himself on me physically. His steadiness, patience, and sense of humor gradually won me over, but it was a struggle for me since my mind had been so resolute not to get married. He eventually shared with me the baggage of his non-Christian days and the guilt he felt when overly pushy, so he was sincerely trying to do life and dating differently by the time he met me.

When I finally said yes to Rob's proposal and we were married, I felt guilty the first few months about being physically intimate. In my head, I knew it was nothing to feel guilty about, but because I'd said *no* for so many years, it was a major shift to all of a sudden say *yes*. We only dated for about six months before getting married and had been careful to not take our physical intimacy too far. Rob was patient with me and didn't push or demand. Our struggle with emotional and physical intimacy didn't express itself until years later.

Eventually, I felt like the only time he would pursue me and give me his undivided attention was when we were having sex. But did I really have his attention? Sometimes, maybe, but I really didn't know what was going on in his mind. When the truth came out about his struggle with pornography, I thought back on those years and wondered.

True intimacy for me really revolved around trust. Can I trust this person with my heart, or will they stomp on it, even if accidentally? I'm speaking in generalities because there are always exceptions, but for most women, good sex is the result of great connection mentally, emotionally, spiritually, and to many men, it is the only way they know how to connect, or it's simply satisfying a physical urge. We couldn't think more differently on this issue. That's why Rob is sharing his thoughts from a man's perspective and I'm commenting from a woman's point of view (at least this woman). With so much shame around the topic of broken intimacy, the discussion is often avoided entirely, and we don't talk about it, leaving us unable to truly understand each other. As a result of this disconnect, we end up with secrets in our lives keeping us sick and further divided.

Owning our distortions

There is general agreement that certain people have addictive tendencies, contributing to increased risk. Rob acknowledges these addictive factors in his life. He was a risk-taker; he was disconnected from emotion; he was apathetic; he was a loner and took his bearings from what others thought of him. Many people appear to be functional but still can't manage their *-ism*. Rob's addictions not only included compromised sexual integrity but also workaholism, status seeking, and compulsive behavior. He acted out sporadically, and even though these unhealthy coping strategies at times became less or went away altogether, they would return when he was unable to manage stress, disappointment, shame, or grief. When you don't learn how to manage emotions, they will manage you in destructive ways.

That's the tricky part about denial. I've heard so many smokers say, "I could stop anytime I want. I just don't want to." But why? If smoking is your go-to way of managing anxiety, even if it works temporarily, of course you would want to keep smoking. We are all in favor of a quick fix or cure. Have a headache? Here's a pill. Something worse? A stronger pill. It takes a bit of know-how and some courage to face our emotions in a healthy way, which becomes a long-term health plan rather than a quick fix.

Most people dislike being labeled, and there really isn't much need for labels unless we can't face reality. Appropriate labels can become categories of understanding that help form pathways to follow as we grow. The label "Adult Child of an Alcoholic" was coined nearly one hundred years ago, and although I don't like owning the label, I needed to face that fact to grow out from under it. If, for example, the label of *shopaholic* is necessary for me to face my unhealthy ways of living, it's worth it. On the other hand, some people use the label as an excuse or a hall pass for bad behavior. Either way requires taking a hard look at our motives for why we do the things we do and our willingness to make changes.

As we mentioned in the chapter on broken trust, what I feared happened. Rob gave in to avoiding, isolating, workaholism, and pornography because of his broken thinking regarding intimacy and as a result of not knowing how to manage stress in a healthy way. I feared being abandoned, and although he never left me physically, we were miles apart in heart and mind. I often wished we could have been helped when we were much younger so we could have had more years of healthy relating, but I'm thankful we eventually found our way to a better place with honesty, forgiveness, and transparency. Shame and fear are such heavy burdens to bear, and we both carried those loads for far too many years. Our hope is that our pain can be useful in your life and our story will help spare you some of the pain of living lives of quiet discontent or giving up all together.

Rob: Intimacy Ignorance... Intimacy Intelligence?

I've already shared the deep influence Larry Crabb had on our journey. When I first met Larry, I knew by his reputation and skill with people there was a high likelihood I wouldn't be able to fool him. He would see through me, like he had X-ray vision for guys like me who were hiding behind a mask. He had worked with hundreds of couples just like us for years, and the closer he got to me, the more my fears were realized. He saw me coming from a hundred miles away. I felt I was wearing a sweatshirt that said, "Clueless," on the front and had flashing Christmas lights around it.

At our first meeting with Larry, we were chatting and getting to know each other, and Roxanne started to cry. Larry quickly and sensitively acknowledged she felt invisible, lonely, and abandoned. Although she minimized these feelings, he saw what was beneath, which is something I had never been particularly good at doing.

Larry turned to me and asked how I thought Roxanne was feeling. He asked if I could see how my behavior triggered memories and wounds from Roxanne's broken family relationships. We talked about what it looks like to love well and what happens when I don't listen, when I don't care for her emotionally, when I'm not present or available. As Roxanne has shared, these wounds were created early in her childhood, long before she ever knew me, but I was touching some of these raw spots. Larry wasn't trying to shame me or blame me. But now, as her husband, I had the opportunity to move toward her with courage, compassion, and understanding to see her as a fellow image-bearer of Christ. He affirmed me for the role I have in her life and that I have the incredible privilege of knowing her in a deep and intimate way that no one else can, other than God Himself.

By allowing her to be alone in our relationship, some would say I had abandoned her and broken our marriage vows. Some might even say this is grounds for divorce. As we spent many more hours together, Larry made it clear how much he supported and defended our marriage covenant, and he was fighting for our survival. He had already identified my "core terror" as feeling weightless, and his intent was to encourage me to wake up and see the gravity of the situation. He has worked with couples a lot stronger than us who didn't make it, and if we didn't want to join the long list of failed marriages, we had some serious work to do.

He also made it clear that we both had a choice. She could choose to hold on to feeling hurt, abandoned, and rejected, and I could choose to continue feeling unwanted, inadequate, and ashamed, or we could accept the invitation to something higher, a relationship not based on broken thinking, expectations, or demands but on a healthy understanding of who God is and who we are. He assured us we weren't alone, and he would join us in the fight.

This became a turning point for us. I started being honest with myself about how I made excuses for not stepping up in the marriage because of what I saw in my parents' roommate-like marriage, my lack of training and experience in healthy expression of sexuality, my belief that love was not freely given but earned, fear of failure, and rationalizing that some secrets are okay. My insecurity of not being able to meet Roxanne's needs perfectly and fear that I was failing at love had paralyzed me and blocked me from doing much of anything. I thought I was protecting myself from failure and pain by not trying.

Intimacy ignorance

A man's heart longs for true intimacy. He deeply desires to know a woman, or any of his closest friends for that matter, truly intimately. The problem is, most men don't have a clue what real intimacy looks like. The men in his life—fathers, uncles, coaches, grandparents, others—have never modeled it for him, abandoning him to his own self-guided journey to understand manhood and masculinity. As already mentioned, most of what is understood as intimacy has been *caught* rather than *taught*, which was true for me as well. Lacking good role models in life who understood true intimacy and masculinity left me watching, waiting, and hoping something would make sense someday or at least create the appearance of intimacy in my important relationships.

Looking carefully at the definition of intimacy, several key characteristics emerge. Intimacy is a combination of closeness (allowing total access to your heart, holding nothing back), privacy (protected and shared only by the two of you), affection (choosing to give and receive love freely and unconditionally), acceptance (loving your partner for who they are, not who you want them to be), and openness (willing to be transparent and vulnerable).

Without a healthy understanding of intimacy, I was groping in the dark, realizing there was so much I didn't understand about this elusive and mysterious concept. I was also afraid someone would see the truth and uncover my intimacy ignorance before I could figure it out.

Most of the men I've worked with over the years share similar stories of how they mentored themselves into manhood, resulting in an unhealthy masculine culture that glorifies a man's power, control, aggression, and competitive nature. This myth of the self-made man compels men to lead lives of isolation, where they become void of deep, meaningful, and intimate relationships. Like many other men, I never asked questions because questions just exposed my intimacy ignorance. I ended up trudging through life harboring an intimacy ignorance that haunted me.

I loved Roxanne with everything I knew about love, but that was the problem. My love knowledge was seriously deficient. I also didn't understand that healthy intimacy is a two-way street meant to be both expressed and received emotionally, intellectually, socially, spiritually, and physically in all our relationships. This is true for men and women. When intimacy is narrowly (and wrongly) defined solely as sexual gratification, it's like pouring water into a bucket with holes. It will never satisfy a man's heart.

It was pivotal for my thinking as I began learning how the influence of healthy intimacy extends beyond just the relationship between a man and a woman. Healthy intimacy in a man's life affects every part of his life and all his relationships. Growing in my understanding of true intimacy, I could see how my intimacy ignorance prepared the soil for the roots of counterfeit intimacy to go deep. My lack of understanding was seriously crippling me, but it didn't let me off the hook for the choices I was making.

Again, this isn't an excuse, but it does offer an explanation. This lack of understanding is one of the major reasons pornography and other unwanted sexual behavior are so rampant. Men are looking for a way to fill the intimacy void in their lives. We are just looking in the wrong places.

Intimacy intelligence

Although I deeply wanted a healthier and more intimate relationship, just wanting this was not enough. The deeply rooted barriers in my life undermining my efforts to develop healthy intimacy needed to be exposed and uprooted. These barriers are my faults, my fears, my failures, and my intimacy ignorance. For a man to truly experience healthy intimacy, he needs all five pillars of intimacy to support it: closeness, privacy, affection, acceptance, and openness. These are inseparable, and each one builds on the other. Each one draws strength and confidence from the others.

I've already said healthy relational intimacy is *not* a one-way street. Healthy intimacy flows back and forth, to and from each other. Both men and women need to learn how to receive intimacy as well as express it appropriately. Healthy intimacy is not developed in isolation. When men are in the grip of counterfeit intimacy, they separate from others and isolate. We no longer see them at church, they avoid men's groups, they reject offers to get together for coffee, and their lives of secrecy become all-consuming.

Men, please hear me on this: you cannot do this on your own. You can read about it, you can talk about it all you want, but in the end, you need to join with other trusted men and purposely, patiently, and persistently practice the skills to develop and strengthen healthy intimacy.

Stages of marriage

In their book *In Quest of the Mythical Mate,*[21] Ellyn Bader and Peter Pearson describe the stages of marriage in a way that helped unlock and expand our understanding of what we were going through in our relationship. They refer to these stages as "Stepping Stones to Intimacy—A Positive Outlook on the Challenges All Couples Face." Understanding that all couples face challenges and go through these various stages helped us see how distorted our view of *normal* was. It also helped shed some light on where we were in these stages and brought clarity to what we needed to improve.

The authors call this a "Positive Outlook" because they view these stages as *normal* and that it's possible to navigate through them to get to a mutually supportive relationship. I was perpetually wanting to be in stage 1, the falling-in-love romantic phase. "Why can't you love me and treat me like you did when we first met?" This is an important stage because it can form a powerful connection, but because of my insecurity and my need (or demand) for connection, I was stuck. As you will see, each stage presents a challenge you must navigate to move on to the next, where two strong individuals form a strong and supportive relationship.

---

[21] Ellyn Bader and Peter Pearson, *In Quest of the Mythical Mate: A Developmental Approach to Diagnosis and Treatment in Couples Therapy* (Routledge, 2014).

Although your spouse or intimate partner might have hurt you deeply, if you can change your conviction that your partner is the source of your unhappiness, if you can understand that struggles are not fatal or a sign of a failing relationship, if you can see your relationship as a journey along a path of development, you will be well on your way to a more positive outlook and hope.

Stage 1: Exclusive bonding—becoming "we"

During this initial blissful merging experience, what began as two individuals now join together into a *we* and *oneness* that take center stage. We focus on what we share and have in common. You're on your best behavior and do everything to show your best side. You experience the ecstasy of giving and being given to by someone who has chosen him or her for his or her own specialness. Your own beliefs, behaviors, and personality might be temporarily suspended for the *we* to become primary. In this stage, your differences are minimized, and your similarities are emphasized.

From this point onward, the balance between two individuals and the *we* will fluctuate due to the struggle between the need for autonomy of the individual and the desire for intimacy of the *we*. Because you are two different individuals, you might not progress through the stages at the same time.

The challenge. During this romantic period, love is somewhat blind. This is a crucial stage as it contributes to forging a strong, exclusive bond based on trust and togetherness. This builds a foundation you can draw upon as your relationship matures.

Stage 2: Managing anxiety over differences

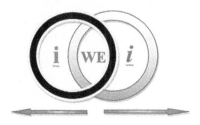

Eventually, each individual reemerges, and differences that might have been dormant begin to emerge. You begin to experience disillusionment and disappointment as you discover your beloved is far from perfect. Shortly after we were married, we could easily identify when we moved into this stage. We started seeing values, desires, and behaviors in ourselves and each other that were irritating and annoying. As we drifted away from each other, we struggled to figure out how much time to be together and when to be alone or with other friends. I'm more extroverted and Rob is more introverted, so I naturally wanted more time with people, and he needed time alone to recharge.

We never saw this tendency in the romantic phase. We always wanted to be together, which suited me just fine, but he put his alone desire on the back burner until we hit stage 2.

This can be a difficult and stressful time, and couples cope differently. Some rise to the challenge by learning more effective ways to deal with differences. Some yearn for the earlier blissful days of stage 1. Most struggling couples try to solve this crisis with two ineffective solutions; Rob and I were no different. In our attempts to return to the comfort of stage 1, we would either hide or deny our differences to avoid conflict or engage in escalating arguments. Rob was usually looking for a way to hide or deny, but at times, it could escalate into anger or stonewalling, both of us hoping to convince the other our opinion was correct.

The challenge. The good news is when couples share a strong compatibility and resilience, these sources of tension and differences hold the greatest promise for personal growth and deepened intimacy. At this stage, you can rise to the challenge and develop effective means of dealing with differences through healthy conflict management and negotiation. These same sources of tension hold the greatest promise of personal growth in your relationship.

Stage 3: Moving from "we" back to "I"— independence and isolation

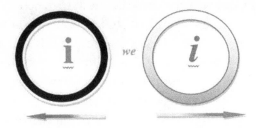

Rob and I were in this stage for a long time. When a couple becomes weary of trying to return to the comfort of stage 1 or just loses heart that it will ever happen, they often become more independent. Often, one pursues, and the other will distance. One may cling to relational connection, and the other pulls away. In our relationship, we went back and forth in the pursuer and distancer roles. At times, I pursued Rob, but as he distanced from me, I became hurt and frustrated and pulled away. When Rob sensed my withdrawal, he would then pursue me, but I pulled further away. As couples continue this back-and-forth dance, an unhealthy independence can emerge, and couples become both physically isolated and emotionally disconnected. At this stage, we were more like roommates than lovers.

In our efforts to reestablish our own identities and self-esteem, the *we* lost its dominance, and the balance shifted heavily back toward the individual. This vital and important stage can present a real crisis for each of you. It could easily look like love and caring have all but disappeared.

At this stage, I'd lost hope we could be a team or mutually supportive, so I got used to doing things alone. Even when I had time to have lunch with Rob, I wouldn't pursue it. I would ask a friend to lunch or read a book as I dined alone with the assumption he wasn't interested.

The challenge. For us, this was the most painful stage, mostly because we didn't know it was a predictable stage that could be conquered, and we had lost hope either of us could change. Most of what we've included in this book are the stepping stones we used to move us through this tough period and into stage 4.

In this stage, you want to learn how to redefine and sustain your identity under stress. This includes healthy boundaries, good listening skills, empathy, and compromise. All this will bring greater richness to your relationship and help form a new foundation for reconnection. Not surprising, this is the stage where most marriages are at risk for divorce. If you don't successfully navigate this stage and learn new skills and ways of relating, you might marry again but will come to this same impasse with the next partner.

Stage 4: Back-and-forth patterns of intimacy

As Rob and I became better at seeing our relationship more like a living, breathing organism, we became more comfortable with togetherness as well as separateness. As we strengthened our own identities, we could come together and maintain our own point of view without hostility, even if the other person disagreed.

We experienced a return to a deeper, more sustainable level of trust and intimacy. When there's been a breach of trust in sexual integrity, your sexual relationship has been affected. Couples who successfully move through this stage often find it accompanied with an enlivened sexual relationship. Though there may be moments of conflict, this is a time when a different quality to the *we-ness* comes into being, one which includes a respect for the existence of two separate individuals.

The challenge. At this stage, you feel much more supported than stifled in your relationship. You hear less "I need" from your partner and more "I would like" or "I really want." It helped us both when we made a request rather than a complaint. When your partner hears a *no* from you, it will more likely be heard as an expression of who you are versus a harsh barb of rejection.

Stage 5: Independence and interdependence

The hallmark of this stage is mutual respect and giving allowances for—or dare I say, celebrate—our differences. It can appear too good to be true, but it's not. Rob and I mostly experience this stage now, with moments of earlier stages. It should be no surprise this level of connection does not happen without effort and being attentive to working through the challenges of each stage. As we increased our abilities to manage our emotional reactions when differences caused tension, our intimacy deepened. In this stage, couples discover they can relate in ways that are true to their most deeply held values and beliefs and they can flow between the individual *I* and the *we* almost automatically. Two individuals now live within the context of the larger *we* without losing their own identity.

As I have done my individual work and Rob has done his, our insecurities have softened. I can ask for help when I need it, and I can stand alone if necessary. Rob has been my biggest cheerleader in this writing project, even though he has revealed things about his history he would have rather kept hidden or avoided altogether. I support him in a healthy way and he supports me when needed.

The challenge. Looking at these stages of intimacy, where is your relationship today? As you might expect, these stages do not unfold in a smooth linear fashion. There will be stress and angst along the way. You may find that you go back and forth between stages at times; we certainly did. But we also want to remind you how important it is to honestly recognize the reality of where you are. Don't be lulled into thinking things just get better on their own. However, be encouraged that your struggle is normal. Problems and disillusionment happen in every relationship. How you think about your difficulties, how you manage your feelings, where you focus your attention, and how you communicate under stress all play a huge role in determining the quality of your relationship.

Roxanne: Our Path to Healing Broken Intimacy

You can't solve it all at once. Microdecisions can lead to macrooutcomes

When we have a gigantic problem, we often think it requires a gigantic solution. As Dan and Chip Heath describe in *Switch: How to Change Things When Change Is Hard*, small, consistent action steps are usually the answer. When learning any new skill or applying new awareness, there is a sense of victory in conquering even a small step along the way. It helps to have a growth mindset and not a fixed mindset as we mentioned before. The problem is, we usually discount the small steps because we think they are insignificant. We then become impatient when, in reality, they are keeping us on the path toward our goal.

In his book *Torn Asunder*,[22] Dave Carder describes how the steps for healing from infidelity seem small, but when joined together, one after another, they are conquering a huge problem. When a trust is broken in any way through infidelity, pornography, secret accounts,

---

[22] Dave Carder, *Torn Asunder: Recovering from Extramarital Affairs* (Moody Publishers, 2008).

secrets of any kind, or betrayal, the problem becomes so big, we can't see a path forward. But small steps toward becoming healthy and accountable are the way forward, even when we are moving more slowly than we'd like at the time. Here are a few examples of baby steps:

Instead of this:	Try this:
Trying to change them	Accept *them* for who *they* are (not necessarily their actions)
Belittling/ Criticizing	Communicate with respect
Seeking their approval	Validate yourself
Making assumptions	Ask questions
Projecting your biases	Listen without judgment
Always giving	Learn to receive
Always saying *yes*	Learn to say *no* based on healthy boundaries

Learn to talk about sex

Couples often argue about sex but rarely talk about it. Consider discussing your insecurities, temptations, fears, and desires. Talk openly about what you are learning. This was hard for both of us for several reasons. Before we could have an honest conversation about Rob's temptations and behavior, we had a difficult conversation about the cloud hanging over this topic that was producing shame and defensiveness. As we worked through the process of forgiveness, we were able to become more transparent and less defensive, and we were able to talk about all forms of intimacy, including sex. When

Rob offered that I could say anything (with gentleness) bothering me, ask questions, or share stumbling blocks, we were able to take small steps to make things more meaningful for both of us. This was huge. It was important for him to give me permission to ask about his temptations and sexual integrity. We were both so used to editing our thoughts and emotions with defensive reactions because of secrecy and shame, we had gotten used to not being truly honest.

Sex and intimacy are not the same thing. Men often view sex as a physical release and a way to connect with their wives, while women tend to see it as an extension of their emotional intimacy and relational connection. Unless we are open to hear and receive each other's perspectives, we remain stuck in our fixed—and often, narrow—opinions. Learning to talk about the differences between intimacy and sex, as well as your perspectives and expectations, is vital.

But let me be transparent here. This is a continuous process, and we don't pretend to be experts in this area. We take it day by day, year by year. What we struggled with in our thirties is not exactly the same as in our sixties. This is an ongoing conversation, and each decade presents its own challenges.

Acceptance

Accept what you can't understand, at least not yet. As a woman, you might never completely understand what your husband experiences regarding sexual temptation. I have an idea, but I still don't know what it's like to have to guard my eyes from seeing a random stranger in a low-cut dress. Some women don't understand how their clothing selections are misunderstood or present temptations. Although you won't fully understand what it's like to be in his skin, he can't fully know what it's like for you either. This is where grace, patience, and forgiveness begin.

I'm not suggesting you accept unhealthy behavior in your move toward acceptance because God loves the sinner but hates the sin. Rather, as we attempt to truly listen and try on each other's perspective with understanding, we are able to have more compassion. From the vantage point of compassion, we make healthier decisions and create better action steps. Acceptance doesn't mean agreement, but it does mean seeing each other through the eyes of God, knowing we are a work in progress, that we are unfinished, at times still wounded, but still deeply loved.

Boundaries

I've heard it said that the most compassionate people are also very clear about their boundaries. This seems so counterintuitive, but boundaries can be an act of love for self and others. So many women I speak with think of boundaries as telling someone else what *they* must do, like "you will never treat me like that again." In reality, it's a choice or action I make based on what is wise and helpful and what is not. Think of a boundary like the property line of your home. You are responsible for taking care of your space in a caring way. You can offer to help fix your neighbor's faucet or mow his lawn, but at the end of the day, he is responsible for his property. What if he is not taking care of his place and you repeatedly do it for him; is that really helpful or loving? It's overstepping to paint your neighbor's house a different color, but we can be guilty of the same when we rescue, indulge, or enable a partner, child, or friend. Nor is it healthy to allow others to make unwise choices for us that affect us adversely.

One boundary I set for myself with Rob and my mother was not being *as* available to process all their complaints or anxieties. I would listen to my mother for hours until I realized I wasn't helping her or myself; in fact, my resentment grew the more she talked. With Rob, he would want to discuss moving or changing jobs when he felt restless, which was hard for me because we moved so many times. So I said, "I'll be happy to talk about this after you have spoken to your wise guy friends first, or when it comes to really making a decision." In time, he learned to manage his restlessness in a healthier way, and he got in touch with the deeper issues when he received the same advice over and over again. We still discussed other things, and I was happy to listen when it helped our relationship grow, but in this area, it was more helpful for him to process his thoughts with another friend.

Once a boundary has been expressed, it still requires making the courageous choice to follow through with it, even if it makes the other person upset. It also requires we respect each other's limits, something many couples struggle with when they are self-focused.

I've worked with couples who have a recurring pattern of getting into fights in the car. After talking about what was wise and helpful, one wife decided to drive separately until they were better at managing their reactivity. A boundary is realizing the only goals I have power and control over are my own. I certainly have influence in the relationship, and I can make requests or establish conditions if bad behavior continues, but I can't make my partner do what I think he should; that's his journey and his choice. If my motive is truly to love my partner and myself, healthy boundaries are part of the process of growth and change when done in a healthy way.

Trust is a process

Anytime a trust has been broken in small or large ways, it is a process to rebuild, and we can't have true intimacy without trust. It helped us to understand that trust is rebuilt in degrees. Love and intimacy may be rekindled as we work to become emotionally safe and trustworthy and increase our respect for each other. We don't quickly jump from forgiveness to a warm feeling of love, no matter how sincere the apology might be.

The people we *feel* love for are usually those we feel the safest with. There's a give and take of full acceptance, and we share common interests and values. Often, we feel this most in the romantic phase of our relationship when everyone is on their best behavior and assuming the best. This is an important period because the foundation of trust builds an alliance, but we can't remain there indefinitely. We replace that phase with the security of a deep friendship with moments of romance. Intimacy becomes the security of knowing I am seen and accepted even if my body is not what it used to be.

I thought Rob and I should remain in the romantic phase, I didn't understand our feelings could wane due to stress or sin, and I wrongly thought if the feelings were gone. they were gone forever.

How many songs have we heard with that refrain? I had an immature understanding of intimacy and relationships. Sure, we hurt one another, and it impacted our ability to forgive and connect, but it wasn't as fatal and final as I assumed.

Trust can be risky

Clearly, trust is important, but it can also be risky. Trust is important in relationships because it invites us to depend on others for love, acceptance, advice, help, support, and a host of other needs and desires. Trust urges us to become vulnerable and to open ourselves to someone else. But trust also involves risk because there is the chance people will not be there for us or that they may not pull through for us because if there were a guarantee we could rely on them to pull through for us, we would not need to trust them.

Therefore, trust can seem dangerous because we risk losing things we value and that are important to us. And when trust is shattered by betrayal, the loss feels great.

Authors, theologians, psychologists, and philosophers have written on the topic of trust for generations, but some of the key qualities of trust that resonate with me include

- being a safe person to share your feelings with,
- being nonjudgmental,
- being positive and quick to give the benefit of the doubt rather than assuming the negative,
- choosing courage over comfort,
- respecting boundaries and limits,
- being able to say no and accept no,
- doing what you say you will do,
- respecting confidentiality,
- taking accountability for your own behavior, and
- making amends when needed.

I trusted Rob in a few of these areas, but there were other places where I was still apprehensive. He was good at keeping confidence, being reliable, and hardworking, but according to these definitions, I didn't trust him in the area of boundaries, being nonjudgmental, or generous. I'm sure he didn't trust me in some of these areas as well. Each area of trust should be carefully considered to avoid making broad generalized statements like, "I don't trust you."

To be fair, we both have areas where we are strong and others that need to be developed, and when we don't clearly define what we're talking about, we run the risk of wrongly making broad judgments about the whole person and miss focusing on specific areas needing growth and change.

We all came into marriage with broken thinking about love and attachments (heck, my closest *person* for years was a dog). We now need to look at what we learned about love. What were those messages we received growing up, and where did they come from? We developed an imprint in our early years of life that formed the ways we interact with others, our ability to develop relationships, and how we experience connection. One of the most important factors in healing broken self-image, broken trust, and broken intimacy is understanding more about these early imprints. We explore this further in chapter 7, "Broken Love Styles."

Discussion Questions

Chapter 6: Broken Intimacy

For personal reflection

1. What descriptions of fear of intimacy do you resonate with and why?
2. In what ways do you resonate with either Roxanne or Rob when it comes to broken intimacy, either emotional, relational, or physical?
3. In the Stepping Stones to Intimacy (the *weI*), identify which stage you are in and why. Write out your thoughts about this.
4. What small steps could you make to build or rebuild emotional intimacy in your relationship? It could start with just being more honest with compassion.

For group discussion

1. How would you define intimacy, and how do you need to redefine this? Write about this and share with your trusted group.
2. In reviewing the qualities of building trust at the end of the chapter, which areas do you need to work on, and which ones would be helpful for you to trust again if your spouse did?
3. How have you defined boundaries? How is it loving to know your limits for yourself and your partner or child.
4. What are you afraid will happen if you set a boundary? Do you believe it's selfish?

CHAPTER 7

Broken Love Styles

When you are with someone day in and day out, you can't hide.
Your weaknesses become quite visible, and old feelings from
the distant past are stirred. The physical nearness of your mate
triggers old feelings as you look to him or her to meet many
of the needs your parents were originally supposed to meet.

—Milan and Kay Yerkovich, *How We Love*

Rob and I had a dysfunctional pattern, an unhealthy dance style, but no one had been able to break it down and show us what to do about it. In my efforts to regain lost connection, I would pursue him, sometimes kindly and sometimes not, and he would distance from me, not wanting or needing the same level of connection. Feeling hurt, I would give up and drift away. In time, he would recognize the gap between us and pursue me because he was uncomfortable with the tension of the divide, overcome with Christian guilt, or it was a reminder of how he was failing.

We frequently see these roles played out in most relationships. One pursues; the other distances. It's a common and discouraging dance we repeated for twenty-five years, like seeing the same depressing landscape out your window and feeling like you're in the movie *Groundhog Day.*

Seeing our distress, God arranged two pivotal experiences that began a healthy shift in our relationship. The two were not related but worked together in giving us a vision for change and growth because we had lost hope we could ever change.

Meeting a mentor

The first was meeting Dr. Larry Crabb, someone who made a lasting impact on both of us. Rob already described his recollection of our first experience with Larry. It was the fall of 2006, and I decided I wanted to attend a weeklong training he hosted three times a year called the School of Spiritual Direction. I had read many of his books in my search for help personally and in our marriage. This conference was designed for pastors and counselors to assist them in their churches and ministries with others. I wasn't attending for the same reasons, although I hoped to glean greater knowledge and understanding. The application process was lengthy, including a required reading list, an essay about your spiritual journey, and a pastor's recommendation. I was motivated to attend because I resonated with Larry Crabb's writing. He so accurately expressed the longings and doubts in my heart, and I was hungry to know more.

Just a few weeks before I was to attend, Rob decided he wanted to go with me. To my surprise, he completed the application process and met all the requirements in short order. I wondered why he wanted to go, but inside, I was grateful for his decision. Although I didn't see it then, this was God's answering my years of prayer.

The day we arrived at this beautiful retreat center in Colorado, the landscape didn't match the strange anxiety I felt inside. Rob was on another wavelength entirely. He put on his professional happy face, working the room, meeting the thirty or so other attendees. I was doing my best to put on a fake smile, be cordial, and mask my rattled nerves. I felt like I was about to go in for major surgery, with an uncertain outcome. I struggled to understand these feelings because we were there with a friendly group of people to learn, nothing was required of me, and we could just receive, or so I thought. I think the Holy Spirit was giving me a heads-up that He was about to rearrange the furniture in my soul.

The evening began with each of us sharing a bit about ourselves, why we were there, where we were from, then Larry began to speak. He was a wonderful combination of insight, knowledge, and warmth, yet he was unnerving at the same time because it felt like he could see right through us. It wasn't his knowledge or credentials that were intimidating but his ability to notice the smallest details, some we were unaware of and some we thought we were hiding.

That first night, he was teaching about the Trinity, a topic some might consider dry theology, but what he was sharing began to water my soul clearly in need of moisture. I unsuccessfully tried to hold back the tears; fortunately we were sitting near the back. Rob was the only one who noticed my tears (and probably Larry). As the evening session wrapped up, Larry extended an invitation to the group that he would meet with any of us privately during our week together if we scheduled a time. Rob decided to take him up on his offer and booked a lunch meeting the next day for the three of us. In a large room with people bustling by getting their lunches, we began to talk. How he got straight to our real issues, I don't know, but he was able to quickly show us he was with us, he cared, and that he saw our issues but no answers just yet.

Most of the people there were individual pastors or counselors; we were the only married couple attending. During our lunch meeting, I think Larry saw our distress and asked if we would be willing to have more conversations with him in front of the class as a teaching tool to help the group. I remember thinking this could be scary and potentially exposing, then I remembered that I came to learn and figured I had nothing to lose. After all, we would never see these people again. How hard could it be?

Over the course of the week, we spent several hours with Larry and in front of the group. He gently opened up and explored things within us we hadn't realized before. He saw and expressed to Rob in vivid pictures the pain I was experiencing, and he privately pointed out my judgmental attitude in the most loving way. He helped Rob see his defensiveness and how he masked his pain and insecurity with humor. He sensitively told Rob he was a good man, but he was weak. He talked about Rob's falling asleep at the wheel of our marriage, and it was time to wake up. He called us each to something higher than just feeling better, getting our desires met, and avoiding pain. In large part, he was a vessel of God inviting us to grow up in Christ. My counselor at home was a Christian, and although empathetic, she never called me to anything higher. In fact, she gave me a hall pass to divorce.

Larry wasn't old enough to be our father, but he became a father figure to us because he represented "the Father" by his love, truth, knowledge, and grace, which was totally different from the example of our earthly fathers. After our time together at the School of Spiritual Direction, God provided several opportunities for us to meet again, and each time was rich with encouragement and insight. As recently as last year, we spent time laughing and sharing with Larry and his wife, Rachael. He went to be with the Lord in 2021 after a lengthy battle with cancer, and although we miss him greatly, I'm excited he is now in the presence of the Lord, completely healed and without sickness or pain. We can't wait to see him and thank him again for the impact he had in our lives.

How we learned to love

The second most helpful concept we learned on our path to healing was uncovering the roots of how we learned to love and attach in childhood from our families. This is called *attachment theory*, and it explains how the most important periods of learning about how we do life and relationships happen within the first ten years. In fact, the brain is neurologically hardwired by how our parents treated us in infancy, making it easier or harder to handle stress or be at peace with ourselves and others. Researchers have found a direct correlation between those early years and how romantic relationships fare later in life. When I first heard this, I was skeptical. How could our childhood experiences have such an impact on our adult relationships so many years later? Don't we eventually grow up and learn what to do and just leave childish ways behind? Unfortunately, the answer is a resounding *no.*

We thought our marriage problems were unique to us, as if we were the only ones who couldn't get our act together. We often hear couples say to us when they have this same unhealthy dance, "We are two good people. We're just not good together." In some cases, that's true, but most of the time, they are stuck in a pattern of relating they learned (or a pattern they used to survive) in childhood, and it's become so automatic and part of who they think they are, it's never challenged.

That was us, and as we delved into our dance and our damaged love styles, we learned there were names to describe these patterns, but more importantly, we learned there was hope of changing. I think we prefer to believe we are like snowflakes, and no two are alike. This is true of our fingerprints but maybe not when it comes to human behavior. Humans are complex, and people cannot be put in a box and labeled with only a few general characteristics. But there are many factors that do influence who we become, like birth order, personality, whether you're an introvert or extrovert, and others. Attachment theory researchers have studied children for over fifty years and found consistent patterns and behaviors that correlate with broken and damaged caregiving experiences in the early years. When the bonding experience with caregivers is broken or damaged in childhood, it shows up later in life.

What is my love style?

We were surprised to find our patterns and ourselves so clearly described in the pages of a book on damaged love styles. How could someone who never met us so accurately describe our pattern? We will give a brief description of five love styles and share which ones we identified with most. As you read these, ask yourself which pattern you identify with. This is summarized because the love styles and patterns we see in relationships are described more fully in the book *How We Love*[23] by our good friends Milan and Kay Yerkovich. Their descriptions of wounded love styles continue to help people around the world.

We highly recommend you check out their book and other resources on *HowWeLove.com* and take the Love Style quiz on their website to help you learn more about your own love style. The title of this book could just as well be called "How We *Don't* Love" because apart from following God's way of relating, we will adopt one of these insecure styles as a means of self-protection.

If you had a difficult childhood or were raised in a particularly abusive family like mine, you may have tried all these styles to survive, which is totally understandable. But now, God wants to free you from these old ways of living and relating. Remember, your love style is not your personality or something you were born with. Rather, it describes the ways you learned to relate because of your experiences growing up. The good news is these damaged love styles can be unlearned.

Am I an avoider?

These people are prone to be hyperindependent. What do they avoid? Vulnerability, emotions, neediness, and honest reflection that bring self-awareness. When they were children, their parents were not tuned into their feelings. As a result, their emotional life is underdeveloped. Receiving limited physical affection and emotional connection, they tend to rid themselves of the anxiety by limiting their need for others. When asked about their childhood, avoiders say, "It was fine," or "My parents taught me a lot." When pressed for details, they have few specific memories.

If you relate to this, you might be thinking, *Darn it! I was sure my spouse was the problem!* You may have survived childhood by detaching from your feelings and needs, but you now need to rec-

---

[23] Milan Yerkovich and Kay Yerkovich, *How We Love: Discover Your Love Style, Enhance Your Marriage* (WaterBrook, 2017)

ognize them to be able to listen to your partner and have a deeper relationship with God.

Am I a vacillator?

The vacillator longs for the kind of intense connection they can *feel.* They are referred to as vacillators because they swing between all good and all bad or all in or all out. Their tendency is to idealize love initially when they feel special and romantically bonded but then devalue others when they are disappointed or their expectations are not met.

What do they expect? They may have grown up in a family where the parents gave sporadic attention, or it was unpredictable, so the conclusions they made are, "To feel secure, I need constant connection and reassurance, even a few fireworks, to know I am loved. Either you are all for me or against me. There can be no in-between." Any signs of moving away, criticism, or mixed messages make Vacillators feel insecure producing reactions of more anger than hurt or sadness.

Am I a pleaser?

If you identify with the pull to please people, especially those closest to you, you may be a pleaser. However, your efforts to please others have more to do with relieving your own anxiety than loving others well. It is likely that your family may have been overly protective or especially critical, so you concluded that things just go better, and I feel better when everyone is happy around me. If those I love are happy, they will be less likely to criticize me or abandon me.

You may have found temporary relief growing up by not rocking the boat, but this isn't the answer because down deep inside, you live on a tightrope of worry about what others think of you. Your tendency is to interpret anyone distancing from you as a sign they are angry or rejecting, and your efforts at giving or appeasing are not sufficient. This can cause you to give even more to calm your own anxiety or to double your efforts to please. Over time, this eventually produces resentment and burnout when your efforts are unappreciated.

Am I a controller or victim?

If you had a chaotic family life growing up (abuse, neglect, violence, drugs, alcohol), where your parents were the source of stress rather than the ones who relieved your stress, you may have concluded that adrenaline and chaos are *normal.* Calmness then equals anxiety because you are waiting for the next storm. Depending on how long it persists or at what age this began, your expectation of relationships becomes distorted.

As a way of relieving your anxiety, you may have struggled with addiction to numb the pain. Some of the expectations in this category are "control or be controlled," or if you identify more as a victim, "If I tried harder in my relationship, my spouse wouldn't get so angry." The victim struggles more with fear, depression, hopelessness, and powerlessness; the controller submerges all these feelings to maintain control or to stay in power. Often, these two styles find each other in marriage because in a strange way, it's comfortable. Both are so out of touch with anger and pain that they have difficulty being open and honest with God and others.

Our particular combination of damaged love styles was Vacillator/Avoider, and because we learned this dance so well, we can still fall back into that pattern. But we've learned to recognize it more quickly, and we know how to get out of it. This is a common combination, and the pattern is predictable. Rob was raised in a home where all conflict and vulnerable emotions were avoided. Before we understood these concepts, I remember how strange it was when we visited his family in Indiana and they only talked about food, the weather, and sports. The dinner table was a sparring match of humor and sarcasm but nothing personal, nothing vulnerable, nothing emotional, and nothing particularly authentic. My childhood was more traumatic, where I saw unhealthy conflict and sometimes violence.

As a result, I had features of many of the damaged love styles having used many of them to survive.

In *our relationship*, I mostly behaved as a vacillator. We see the vacillator/avoider combination most frequently with couples seeking counseling, and it accurately describes our pursuer-distancer dance. Over the years as we have talked to groups about our pattern, couples inevitably seek us out to tell us, "We're just like you," with astonished looks on their faces. It's like finally being diagnosed with a disease no one could figure out. The good news is for each of these damaged love styles, there are growth goals and new ways to relate in more secure ways, and if a couple is willing, this can turn a relationship around. You don't have to stay stuck, but change takes intentionality, courage, and action.

> Several other combinations are described in *How We Love*, but we have provided the Vacillator-Avoider core pattern in the appendix. This is one of the most common combinations in relationships. You may be relieved to see you are not alone.

As a vacillator, I was looking to Rob to complete me, to fill the hole of abandonment. As a result, I was mostly *pleasing* in the early stages of our marriage to earn or secure his love for me but often not speaking up or having clear boundaries when upset. When my efforts to please didn't work, I flipped to devaluing him and pulled away out of hurt and anger. In general, the vacillator can swing from being loving and pleasing initially, and then when disappointed, they become judgmental, critical, and often shut down emotionally. This is confusing for their mate, making the partner more anxious and wondering what reaction they'll receive. They feel they are walking on eggshells.

As I began to connect the dots of my trauma to my adult insecurities and reactions, my codependent tendencies were highlighted. I never fully understood the term *codependent*. It sounded like a term for weakness and for those who couldn't do things for themselves, which didn't fit me. I've since learned it means so much more. It includes being overly influenced or dependent on someone else to find my identity, direction, choices, peace, and boundaries. Here is a brief list of some of the features of codependency.

Features of Codependency

Having a hard time saying *no*	Feeling a need to be liked by everyone
Having poor boundaries	Feeling a need to always be in a relationship
Showing emotional reactivity	Denying one's own needs, thoughts, and feelings
Feeling compelled to take care of people	Having intimacy issues; confusing love and pity
Need for control, especially over others	Fixating on mistakes
Difficulty communicating honestly	Displaying fear of abandonment

Ideally, secure individuals who are not codependent have a clearer view of themselves and their worth, and they are better able to love well by being honest, authentic, and less reactive. When we were both looking for confirmation of our worth from each other to feel secure, we couldn't love well. If you knew your net worth was five hundred million dollars and you were satisfied with it, you would live more securely and be less worried if someone tried to cheat you out of a dollar.

Path to healing

The first step in any endeavor is to know where you are before you can move forward. It's like when you go to the mall and stand in front of the directory to get your bearings. What's the first thing you see? The big red dot that says, "You Are Here." To see where we were meant, we needed to be open to honest self-examination. The path to healing our broken love styles was no different. Our styles were quite different, but because we identified with these descriptions, it gave us hope for a way forward.

I became less judgmental of Rob because I could see this was not an uncommon style. He was taught to avoid and wasn't the only one who avoided. The pieces also fell into place when I thought back on some of the things Larry shared with us. I was insecure and overly judgmental, and Rob was asleep at the wheel, avoiding conflict or failure. Awareness of these patterns alone wasn't the answer, but it gave us hope.

Next, we individually started working on our own *stuff*. Some of my growth goals were to become less black-and-white or all good/all bad, and to lower my high expectations of myself, Rob, the kids, a vacation—you name it. I began taking my thoughts and emotions to the Lord and aligning my views with my true identity rather than the scared, insecure little girl who was afraid of abandonment. This helped me connect the dots of the past to my responses in the present.

I worked on lowering my emotional reactivity, and Rob worked on recognizing his emotions. For a long time, he carried a feelings word sheet around to help identify what was happening inside. It's not that he wasn't feeling; he had just learned to bury them so deeply he couldn't see them or feel them. As we both looked at our childhoods, we didn't look just at the facts but how those events affected us and the conclusions we made. We had different perspectives and started seeing things we had minimized and labeled as *normal* that were not all that *normal*. I looked for the emotions underneath my anger—which were usually hurt, sadness, or shame—to discover the sensitivity being triggered.

Recognizing our reactivity, learning a new vocabulary of feeling words, and seeing the impact of the past on our present took time, and like peeling the layers of an onion, God continues to give new awareness. I'm sure we wouldn't be able to take it if he showed us all at once. Because we are not machines in need of fixing but rather people in need of growth in the context of relationships, there's not a one-and-done mindset or cure. We are all in process on this side of heaven, and healthy growth usually comes in baby steps not in giant leaps.

We adopted a mindset of humility and continued working on our *relationship* dance together. We took ballroom dancing lessons a few years ago, which revealed our pattern in a different way. No matter the dance style—waltz, two-step, cha-cha, or foxtrot—I had trouble following, and Rob had trouble leading. It didn't help that I had experience with dance all the way through college, and Rob never danced a day in his life. With this combination, I was unconsciously leading, or at least predicting, his moves and quick to *suggest* when he was doing it wrong.

The instructor, seeing our frustration, asked me to close my eyes and go by *feel* more than trying to execute the correct dance steps, and he asked Rob to think ahead a few steps, so he knew where he was going and could lead us to the next move. As we were getting better at the two-step, we learned to move together rather than against each other, and we each had different skills to practice and master.

The same is true of our relational dance style. We each became more self-aware, learning to apply new habits individually, and finally putting the two together in a meaningful way through healthier communication.

In the appendix, we have included our unhealthy Avoider-Vacillator dance pattern for your review because this is the most common combination among couples. It's important to note, this is not about gender. We see both male and female equally distributed among these love styles. Take a look and see if it fits you. There are too many other combinations to describe in this book, but they are explained in detail in the book *How We Love*.

There is a sixth category of Attachment, referred to as the *Securely Attached*, and only about 20 percent of the population fits this category. These are fortunate folks who learned the building blocks of healthy relating from their first family and usually fare better in their adult relationships. Here's a brief list of qualities of the securely attached individual. The good news is, even if we didn't learn these skills early in life, they can still be learned as adults.

Securely attached

- You tend to have good self-esteem and do not *depend* on validation from others to feel better.
- You have trust in your relationships until given a valid reason not to.
- You have a wide range of emotions and express them appropriately.
- You can ask for help and receive from others when you have needs instead of trying to deal with stressful situations on your own.
- You understand your needs and can draw healthy boundaries around them.
- You can provide support to others when needed.
- When you make mistakes, you can grieve, learn, and move forward.
- You know how to give and receive comfort.
- You know how to wait.
- You know how to listen without reactivity.
- You can say *no* to others even when you know it might upset them.
- You are adventuresome and know how to play and have fun.
- You know you're not perfect and give your loved ones room to disagree.

Couples who are securely attached experience interdependence—meaning, they can receive support from their partner as well as give support. They know how to come together in a meaningful way but can also be apart in a healthy way. They can be okay emotionally, even when their partner might be struggling and can still be caring and concerned without feeling anxious or pressure to fix something.

It's necessary to have a vision of what this type of relationship looks like since so many of us didn't see this growing up. But knowledge alone doesn't change things; it takes humility, accountability, and action with the help of God to make lasting changes.

In the next chapter, we will attempt to break into the area most couples say is their core issue: communication. While it's true that communication suffers when a relationship suffers, simply thinking we need to learn to communicate better is a knee-jerk reaction and an oversimplification of a complex topic. Stay with us.

ROXANNE AND ROB MARONEY

Discussion Questions

Chapter 7: Broken Love Styles

For personal reflection

1. If you haven't done so yet, take the Love Style test on *HowWeLove.com*.
2. Which style or styles did you score the highest?
3. As you review your potentially broken love style, what are your thoughts and feelings?
4. On a scale of one to ten, how open are you to learning more about relating to others and yourself in a different way?
5. Connect the dots. Although you are not responsible for your spouse's choices, you each brought damaged love styles into your marriage. How has yours affected your relationship?

Group discussion questions

1. Read the list of codependent characteristics and check any that fit you. Then look at the description of the securely attached love style at the end of this chapter and pick one or two to work on. Share with your group what you are learning about your love style.
2. Review the Vacillator-Avoider diagram in the appendix to see if your marriage fits this dance pattern. There are other combinations of love styles, and we highly recommend buying the book *How We Love* by Milan and Kay Yerkovich for detailed explanations of each style and how they combine in relationships.

CHAPTER 8

Broken Communication

May the words of my mouth and the meditation of my heart
be acceptable to You, Lord, my rock and my redeemer.

—Psalm 19:14 (CSB)

As I am writing now, we have been married forty-six years. This gives me several decades to reflect on and to review—too much to include here. Fortunately, I've kept journals over the years that take me back to certain periods, what I was struggling with, where we were living, what was happening between us. I pondered what went wrong, what was most impactful or helpful, and what the best practices were for our relational healing.

When speaking to groups, we often ask the question, "What do you struggle with most in your marriage?" Ninety percent of the time they answer *communication*, which was true of us as well. But communication struggles are not just about the mechanics of knowing *how* to communicate; it's more about our *reactivity* to what's being said that gets in the way of truly hearing each other. Sure, we can improve our communication skills, but we also need to get better at monitoring what's happening on the inside.

When counseling couples, I've observed they comprehend the *how-tos* of change easier than making the decision they *want* to change. That's why we tackled our triggers and reactivity first. If we don't become aware of our land mines of reactivity (the bombs that go off when we're just talking about making coffee), it will be nearly impossible to apply best practices of communication in more sensitive areas. As I share our struggles, I will reveal our communication trials, as well as the ways we found to connect on a more meaningful level.

If I painted a picture of our talks over the years, it would look like a poker game, except I don't really like playing poker, and Rob is a master. I would prefer everyone to show their cards and give money to the person with the best hand. But Rob liked the challenge of winning and playing his cards close to his chest. I wanted to talk about things on an emotional level, but he was more like an attorney debating the facts.

As we've shared in previous chapters, in my frustration and fatigue, I would eventually give up and walk away. He would then pursue me because he couldn't tolerate the tension of the silence. This pattern was repeated over and over again, chasing each other like the old Pac-Man video game. I pursued him with complaints; he distanced. Then I turned and distanced, feeling frustrated and rejected. As the gap between us grew larger, he pursued me out of guilt. Sound familiar? Most couples we've worked with have a pursuer-and-a-distancer dance in one form or another, which are the ingredients of an unhealthy relational style.

Roxanne's Journal—November 25

Relationally I feel we are cordial but distant, when we do talk the listening is still defensive. His tone of voice sounds impatient and parental, kind of bossy, although he accuses me of the same. I'm not feeling drawn to him when I'm saying how I feel because he disputes my usage of certain words. There is little touch, and we behave as neighbors, we've lost fun and excitement. I wonder if there is some sense of competition, not cooperation when we are with the counselor. Even there, I think he's faking it, coming off so nice and reasonable. Maybe we should both just do our own thing. He wants to go back to school, and I'll find a way to be happy and challenged separately. Please help God, we are not happy.

When I wrote these words, I knew further distance between us wasn't the answer; I just didn't have a clue how to improve the situation. We were both living reactively, and we weren't secure enough to listen to each other with compassion or even to be polite at times. If someone had given us the *how-tos* of communication, I doubt we would have been able to apply them; there was a ticking bomb between us.

A book published years ago by Robert Fulghum entitled, *All I Really Needed to Know I Learned in Kindergarten.*[24] Fulghum explores how the skills learned at that young age are applicable throughout life. For example, when someone is talking, you listen; when you want to speak, you raise your hand and don't interrupt. Other topics were "play fair," "don't hit," "put things back where you found them," "share," and "say you're sorry when you hurt someone." We all know these skills, or at least we heard them in kindergarten, but when we became adults, we threw it all out, especially when it comes to communication.

For at least twenty years, I asked Rob to repeat back what I said when we were having a discussion or a difference of opinion. Even if he disagreed, at least I would know he heard me. His response was usually "I heard you. I'm not an idiot," further widening our divide. Something prevented him from hearing my request that neither of us could understand. "Repeating back" what the other person said was not a skill we had mastered. In our unhealthy communication pattern, I would share but not feel heard (touching a wound from my

---

[24] Robert Fulghum, *All I Really Need to Know I Learned in Kindergarten: Uncommon Thoughts on Common Things* (Ballantine Books, 2004).

family history), causing me to be hypersensitive and quick to judge. This caused Rob to be on high alert for feeling like a failure or for getting it wrong (touching a wound from his family history). As his anxiety rose, his listening skills went down, making it harder for him to reflect back what I had said.

I continued to feel unseen and unheard for years. Whenever Rob heard me say, "We need to talk," he felt like he was back in junior high walking into class and the teacher announcing a pop quiz, which of course he was not prepared for and sure to fail. I was much more concerned with being heard and understood; Rob was much more concerned about feeling like a success and avoiding failure. When we couldn't connect with each other and communication became a chore, we drifted apart and stopped trying. He found his purpose and affirmation in work, and I found purpose and meaning in ministry and relationships with girlfriends who understood me. But under the surface there was a simmering anger and resentment I kept hidden, even from myself, sometimes reflected in my dreams.

Journal—May 28

> I had a dream last night, and it was an argument with Rob in the rain in a parking lot. He took offense to something I said, and I lost it. It was the culmination of all the times he was so hyper-sensitive and self-centered, and telling me what to do because he knows best. All we talk about with friends are *his* plans. When I ask for what I need, he argues with it. Am I as mad as I was in the dream? The thoughts it triggers in me are "I'm unimportant, I'm forgotten, I'm only useful, and I need some space."

If we could have only talked about what was going on inside at that time, we could have spared each other so much pain, suffering, and loneliness. We just didn't know how, and we were guilty of wanting to change each other, focusing more on receiving than giving.

In our marriage vows many years before, we promised to "have and to hold from this day forward, for better, for worse, for richer, for poorer, in sickness and in health, to love and to cherish, till death do we part, according to God's holy law." In reality, we had no clue what we were promising. We said those words, but inside, we were each saying something vastly different. Since we were only in our early twenties and fairly new Christians, we were largely influenced by our family histories more than our faith and commitment to Christ. I was promising to romantically love Rob and be in awe of him if he did the same for me, and Rob's promise was to love me as long as I made him feel good about himself. As a man, he understood promising to provide and protect, but other than physical care, he had no idea what it meant to cherish. He was living out what he saw in his first family. His dad went to work, and Mom did everything else. No one spoke about their feelings or pursued the interests of each other. Some years into our marriage, I remember telling Rob I feared we were turning into Bob and Doris (his parents). He quickly dismissed the thought, saying, "We aren't like them." But I saw the resemblance more and more as time went on.

There was a terror inside both of us driving most of our decisions. I feared being invisible and abandoned, and he feared being a failure, weightless, and ashamed. Those terrors were like a giant elephant in the room, and we awkwardly maneuvered around him in every conversation. The first step in our communication repair was learning to talk about our histories and listening with compassion, not only for each other but also for ourselves.

Rob: The Power of Being Present

The opposite of talking is not listening…
the opposite of talking is waiting.[25]

---

[25] Fran Lebowitz, *The Fran Lebowitz Reader* (Vintage Books, 1964).

In her book *The Listener*, Taylor Caldwell writes,

> The most desperate need today is not a new vaccine for any disease, or a new religion, or a new way of life. Man does not need to go to the moon or to other solar systems. He does not require bigger and better bombs and missiles. He will not expire out of frustration if he is not able to buy the brightest and newest gadgets. His real need, his most terrible need, is for someone to listen to him, not as a patient, but as a human soul.[26]

Waiting, being patient, being present, being attentive to another person—these are all skills I missed growing up. Not only did I not know how to really listen to others, but I also didn't realize my own need to be heard either. In my family, everyone took care of themselves, and I didn't rely on anyone else to help me work through any troubling thoughts, feelings, or emotions. The lesson I learned growing up was be responsible for yourself; you're on your own. With that belief as my compass to guide me, why would I have a need for others? Having rarely experienced being heard myself, why would I recognize being heard as a legitimate desire or need in someone else? I came into marriage with a limited communication skill set, but beyond my lack of communication competency, I also had broken thinking about how communication and intimacy even fit together.

Being present and attentive to someone else means waiting and being silent at times. But waiting is more than just being silent, and the most effective kind of silence requires more than just not talking. I was often preoccupied with a hundred different things at the same time, which, as you can imagine, got in the way of being present in conversations. When I am preoccupied worrying about solving prob-

---

[26] Taylor Caldwell, *The Listener* (Doubleday & Co., Inc., 1960).

lems that may not yet exist or forming a response in my mind, I can't be present or attentive to Roxanne or anyone else for that matter.

When my mind is overwhelmed with activity and buzzing with internal noise, even if I am outwardly silent, I notice only things that promise immediate satisfaction of my own self-focused interests. I often stop listening, interrupt, and start "spouting off" something that seemed important at that time. I've worked with many men who share the common experience of "tuning out" in conversations, as they are busy thinking about what they want to say next rather than listening to the person in front of them. It's what Roxanne called "going ghost." This is how she described being with me when she knew I really wasn't present. She says it's like being with a *ghost* of Rob. He's kind of present but also kind of *see-through-ish*. She could tell when I was present and when I wasn't, and believe it or not, your partner can tell too.

In contrast, nurturing an inner silence creates space that allows for greater sensitivity to subtle aspects of communication that are often lost or overlooked. When I practice this kind of inner silence, I not only hear the words being said, but I also become more attuned to those important clues between the words being said.

Spouting off before listening to the facts is
both shameful and foolish. (Proverbs 18:13 CSB)

Knowing whether you are more introverted or extroverted is helpful in understanding yourself. On introvert-extrovert scale, I fall close to the middle but slightly more introverted than extroverted. At times, too much contact with people can become overwhelming for me, and I need solitude to reenergize. I knew how to be alone and be still, but it took time, discipline, and practice for me to learn to be still, to practice being silent, to stop my internal engine long enough to listen, focus, and be present for the person sitting in front of me. The practice of stillness and solitude does not mean isolating and retreating. Simply "going away" without a specific intent to listen and replenish often leads to continued rumination over what I'm stressed about.

When my mind gets busy working on things other than what's happening in the moment, I miss a lot and often deceive myself into thinking I am being a good listener. Roxanne knew when I was not being present, and I would predict that your partner can tell when you've checked out too. Paying attention and listening well is not easy and not always convenient, but attentiveness is most needed when it is least convenient. This is a core relationship skill worth paying attention to and well worth improving.

Roxanne: Our Path toward Healthy Communication

Becoming aware of our sensitivities, triggers, and poor habits, we started *learning and applying* some of the dos and don'ts of communication. We've found that consistently applying small steps can move you in the right direction. The couples we work with who don't apply these tips and continue self-sabotaging habits behind closed doors find themselves stuck and frustrated. Remember, insanity is doing what you've always done and expecting different results.

Barriers to healthy communication

1. Being quick to give advice before understanding and empathy

The average person listens for around thirty seconds before forming a reply in their head. It's a habit because most of us are more interested in giving our opinions than offering understanding. Good listeners set aside their needs and tune in to the other person. It's an active process of passing the ball back and forth. The temptation is to talk about our own experience as a teaching tool with comments like, "That reminds me of a time when…" Everyone has their own story to tell, but I often minimized Rob's struggles because they didn't seem as hard compared to mine.

I hated it when Rob interrupted and offered his opinion before he heard what I was saying. We encourage couples to learn to become "generous listeners"—meaning, letting your partner know you heard them and suspending your comments until they are done. All too frequently, conversations become a ping-pong match of opinions, which is basically a debate.

Here's an example of our communication breakdown. In the early years of our marriage, we spent two years traveling the United States and Canada in a thirty-five-foot travel trailer as part of a ministry conference team. During the second year, I had a baby, and we continued to travel with her. The trailer was relatively nice, but it was like living in a hallway, and the farthest I could get from our crying baby was about thirty feet.

One of our stops during this time was in northern Indiana. We were parked on a small college campus where we were conducting a conference. It was in the dead of winter, and everything seemed safe enough until I heard on the news a blizzard was coming. I'm a California girl with a new baby. Our trailer was nothing more than a long metal box, and I'd never been in a blizzard before, so I shared my fears and worries about what could happen with Rob. Since he was from the Midwest, he shrugged off my concerns and said "It's just snow with a lot of wind. We'll be fine."

As it turned out, it was a major weather event, burying roads and cars and forcing the Indiana National Guard to get involved. People still talk about the winter of 1978 in "those parts." By God's grace, we made it through, and even though Rob had no control over the weather, it would have been more comforting if he had listened with more compassion, heard my anguish, and assured me we would face it together.

Many times, I wasn't asking for advice, just a listening ear and a bit of compassion. But because he thought his appointed duty was "the fixer," he offered advice too quickly with little empathy or validation first. I've worked with couples who express, "That's just not me. I'm not the touchy-feely type," which may be true. Most likely, they never learned sensitivity as kids, so their approach to relationships is like being loud and rough around a baby and concluding, "I'm just not good with babies."

What if your approach needs to change? What if you could apply some new skills to improve all your relationships, including babies? A few well-chosen words at the right time can remarkably change your relationship. Some people need help learning this, and that's where effective counseling and coaching come in.

In his book *People Fuel*,[27] Dr. John Townsend offers excellent insight into the essential nutrients all relationships need to grow in a healthy way. He identifies four quadrants with twenty-two healthy qualities necessary for the building of great relationships. Using this tool with clients, I ask them to identify which box they go to when having a conflict or conversation. Those who have the most trouble start their interactions in quadrants 3 or 4. They are quick to give advice or instruction without first expressing care or concern. All four quadrants are necessary, but John makes the case for starting in quadrant 1, then moving to quadrant 2, and lastly to quadrants 3 and 4. Depending on the conversation, it's not necessary to touch on every point in each quadrant, but these are twenty-two nutrients Townsend notes as the most necessary in communication.

---

[27] John Townsend, *People Fuel* (Zondervan, 2019).

Four Quadrants of Relational Nutrients

In Order from 1 to 4

Quadrant 1: Be Present	Quadrant 2: Convey the Good
Acceptance: Connect without judgment. *Attunement*: Be aware of what another is experiencing and respond to it. *Validation*: Convey that a person's experience is significant and not to be dismissed. *Identification*: Share your similar story. *Containment*: Allow the other to vent while staying warm without reacting. *Comfort*: Provide support for someone's loss.	*Affirmation*: Draw attention to the good. *Encouragement*: Convey that you believe in someone's ability to do the difficult. *Respect*: Assign value. *Hope*: Provide reality-based confidence in the future. *Forgiveness*: Cancel a debt. *Celebration*: Acknowledge a win, both cognitively and emotionally.
Quadrant 3: Provide Reality	Quadrant 4: Call to Action
Clarification: Bring order to confusion. *Perspective*: Offer a different viewpoint. *Insight*: Convey a deeper understanding. *Feedback*: Give a personal response. *Confrontation*: Face someone with an appeal to change.	*Advice*: Recommend an action step. *Structure*: Provide a framework. *Challenge*: Strongly recommend a difficult action. *Development*: Create a growth environment. *Service*: Guide engagement to giving back.

Quadrant 1: Be Present; start with acceptance, validation, comfort, and attunement in words and body language. Next, move to

Quadrant 2: Convey the Good; encourage the person by offering respect, hope, and belief in them. These comments are not minimizing the situation but expressing confidence and hope. Next, move to *Quadrant 3: Provide Reality*. This is where you can offer statements like "I wonder if this is what's happening," to bring clarity, perspective, and even confrontation if change is necessary. Lastly, move to *Quadrant 4: Call to Action*. It's always preferable to ask questions here, like "What do you think you need?" rather than offering your opinion. If asked, this is where you could offer recommendations, steps forward, or help with a difficult choice. If you start the conversation in quadrant 4, there's usually little empathy or a sense the listener cares. There is a time for advice but not before first expressing care and empathy. This is true with all relationships, especially with kids. Look at the chart and ask yourself where you usually start your conversations with your kids or spouse. This flowchart helped us recognize some bad habits of jumping to conclusions and giving unwanted advice too quickly.

2.   Being distracted or not present

Effective communication doesn't happen in a sports bar, with phones in hand, or when you are mentally preoccupied. It takes practice and the right environment to focus on active listening. This skill can also be learned and developed. In the early years, I was distracted by the kids and the endless list of things to do, while Rob was more preoccupied with work. Raising a family with small children, running from one sport to the other, to and from school, we felt overcommitted. It seemed like there was never a good time to talk. We hear this complaint from so many couples, but if you believed active listening could turn your relationship around, would you be willing to rearrange things to make space for each other?

As the years went by and the kids were around less and less, we saw how empty our communication was because we hadn't practiced being present with one another. To be a generous listener takes self-control, willingness, and the right environment. Go for a walk without the kids, have coffee at the harbor, turn off the TV in your bedroom, have dinner together, listen the way you want to be listened to. These are the ingredients of being present and not distracted.

3. Being quick to judge, criticize, or lead with sarcasm

We all have expectations that lead us to judge others. I've heard it said that an expectation is a resentment waiting to happen. These assumptions make us hypersensitive or only able to hear what we want or expect to hear. Some of the expectations we bring to conversations are built up from our history as a couple and some from our earliest relationships. More than we like to admit, we continue to live in the shadow of the families we grew up with. Rob's family used sarcasm as a sport. I was more prone to judge or criticize because of my family. We all need to become aware of our biases and unhealthy expectations and where they came from.

I recently heard a podcast from Brené Brown—author, researcher and speaker—on the issues of shame and resilience. To paraphrase, she shared how we all form beliefs and opinions about life and ourselves. We then unconsciously go about collecting data to support that viewpoint. Even if we come to a horrible conclusion like, "I'm worthless," we still look for data to support that belief and negate or not notice evidence to the contrary. I concluded *people don't change* because I was influenced by a mother who didn't change. Instead of being influenced by stories of people who healed or made huge changes in their lives, I zeroed in on the ones who didn't.

This human tendency of being fixed in our opinions based on the data we've gathered from our experience causes much of our judgments and criticism. When Rob and I weren't open to other data, we kept banging our drum of opinion demanding the other see it our way.

4. Being defensive and reactive

One of the biggest reasons people don't listen is they become emotionally reactive. If we're not aware of our triggers, we often react and don't know why. We think it's our kids or partner, but when we see our anger as a clue of something inside that needs healing, we're able to listen with less defensiveness and reactivity. I was sensitive to being marginalized, mostly because I was the runt of the litter growing up, and my thoughts or opinions weren't listened to or considered. So if Rob was quick to dismiss my suggestions or opinions, I was quick to get angry and express it wrongly. Of course, it's important to at least consider each other's thoughts and emotions, even if we don't agree, but reactivity from unhealed places makes this almost impossible when we are so focused on defending ourselves.

Here's a list of the most common ways we defend ourselves. Read through these and see which ones you use to protect yourself or keep others from getting too close and potentially hurting you.

- *Regression*: If I'm angry or hurt, I sometimes revert to childish ways, sulk, leave, or have temper tantrums.
- *Suppression*: I distract myself so I don't have to feel what's bothering me. I work at erasing unpleasant experiences.
- *Withdrawal*: When I'm hurt or upset, I physically leave or go off in my own thoughts.
- *Blame*: Other people cause most of my problems. I act and feel the way I do because of them; if they would change, I would be fine (a very common choice).
- *Projection*: I assume others are thinking and feeling the same way I am (guilt, anger, distrust).
- *Rationalization*: It's easy to tell myself the wrong things I do aren't as bad when compared to what most people do wrong.
- *Devaluation*: When I'm upset, I focus on the negative traits in others, which are always more numerous or pronounced than my own.
- *Intellectualization*: I can analyze my way out of any feeling or emotion.
- *Compensation*: I emphasize my good points to hide my deficiencies ("I may have lied, but at least I don't drink").
- *Denial*: I refuse to look at reality, pain, or problems and call it having a positive attitude.

- *Replacement*: When I'm feeling a negative emotion, I express the opposite to hide the truth (acting calm when you're angry or smiling when you're sad).
- *Distraction*: I avoid conflict or pain by filling my day with any task; I stay busy.

As an avoider, Rob leaned more heavily on suppression, withdrawal, and denial. As a vacillator, I was more inclined to blame, projection, and devaluation. But the source of them all is reactivity from our broken love styles, insecurity, and sometimes just plain sin.

5. Other bad habits

- *Interrupting or interrogating.* The person who starts a sentence should be the one who finishes it.
- *Mind reading.*
- All-or-nothing statements like, "You always," or "You never."
- *Stonewalling or walking away*, without trying to repair later.

Building blocks for healthy communication

1. *Concentrate on the person speaking.* Set aside distractions. If it's difficult for you to pay attention, take notes.
2. *Suspend your agenda.* Set your ego aside and just be curious without fixing or minimizing.
3. *Interrupt as little as possible.* If you do interrupt, it should be to encourage the speaker to say more or to validate them.
4. *Listen* to grasp what the speaker is saying.
5. *Don't react* to just the words; listen for the underlying ideas, feelings, and beliefs.
6. *Try to put yourself in the other person's shoes.* This is really hard if no one ever did this for you growing up, but the more you practice this, the better you will be at it.

7. *Pay attention to their body language* as a clue to how they are feeling. Look them in the eye with interest; 80 percent of communication is nonverbal.

8. *Let the speaker know you understand.* Don't just say, "I understand." Repeating back what you heard confirms you were really listening and shows you are present. It doesn't have to be word for word, but it should be free of your perspective and opinions.

9. *Offer empathic or reassuring comments.* If you can't think of any, you can Google "Empathetic and Validating Statements." Tons come up.

10. *Use open-ended questions or statements*, like "Tell me more," or "What else?" or "How did this affect you?" Avoid asking *yes* or *no* questions. This should be a question you truly don't know the answer to and not an attempt to manipulate toward a particular agenda or conclusion you desire.

11. Some couples have found it helpful to *use a timer* to control detours or avoid rabbit trails. Set it for fifteen minutes to be the listener and then trade places.

Advice for the speaker

1. *Calm yourself first.* How a conversation starts is how it will end; if you come in hot, it will end hot. When you have a reaction, the first pulse you need to take is your own. Take a moment to pray and reflect and then continue with a softer start using I statements of ownership first. If you would like something from your partner, make a request, not a complaint, such as, "I know I can be sensitive in this area, but I was confused when you didn't call the other night. It helps me when you let me know you got there safely."

2. *Timing and reactivity.* Don't start with, "We need to talk." There may not be a perfect time to talk in our busy lives, but there are better times than others, like when your partner is not tired or stressed. Example: "I've been struggling

184

with something, and you don't need to fix it. I would just like to process it with you. Is this a good time to talk? If not, when would be a good time for you?"

3. *Stay on topic.* A pattern we often see with couples, and we were guilty of as well, is a form of "crazy making." I would come to Rob with topic *A,* and he would switch it to topic *B,* usually as a form of defensiveness, and topic *A* is lost altogether. Be willing to bring the conversation back to topic *A* if this happens. A way to keep on track is to use the word *nevertheless.* It might not be a word you use often, but when it comes to communication, it's especially useful. For example, when my kids were teens, I would ask them to pick up their dirty dishes. The response was sometimes, "Oh, Mom, you're just a clean freak." The temptation was to defend myself (which would be topic *B*), but instead, I would say, "Nevertheless, please pick up your dishes."

4. *Be clear.* A common conflict we hear from couples is lack of communication about time. The request from either of them could be, "Would you call or text to let me know when you'll be home?" If the answer comes back with another topic like, "Why do you need to know?" or "You're too uptight," you are switching topics, which takes the conversation in circles. Instead, the reply could be, "Maybe so, nevertheless I would still like to know when you will be home." Of course, tone of voice is all important, and how it's delivered can be matter-of-fact or confrontational.

5. *Don't overwhelm with too many words.* Use periods and pause so your partner can repeat back. Some people have far more words than others and can overdescribe in our attempt to make a point and be heard. It's okay to have lots to say, but share in smaller doses so it can be digested and not overwhelm your spouse. Using periods and pauses can help you breathe so you can both stay more connected and calm.

Don't get discouraged; keep trying

A sample "Connecting Conversation" is included in the appendix as a suggested guide to help you get started. There are many ways to have a connecting conversation. We recommend you start with a guide like this to help you become more comfortable and able to have conversations that don't escalate or go in circles.

Being able to have a conversation where you feel heard and connected with one another is important in any relationship. But if your relationship is in crisis or stressed in any way, as it is when trust has been broken, it becomes even more critical for both of you to learn and practice this healthy conversation skill. Don't be discouraged if you don't do it perfectly the first time. One of the most generous gifts you can give each other is a "do-over." Don't be afraid or unwilling to say, "That didn't go well. Can we try that again?" We worked on this for a long time and continue doing so.

People approach change in their lives in a variety of ways. Some of the ways we try to change might work, but other times, they don't. Sometimes, change lasts awhile, but without a true change of heart, we return to old patterns. A huge component of creating and sustaining healthy change comes down to a change of heart. Most of the time, we need more than a *how-to* manual with step-by-step instructions. We had read a lot of books, attended a lot of marriage workshops, and seen a lot of counselors. We were looking for more than another *technique*.

Understanding how a change of heart really happens means looking more closely at some of the ways we tried to change that didn't work and then exploring a completely different approach. In this next chapter, we'll talk about the kind of change that lasts.

Discussion Questions

Chapter 8: Broken Communication

For personal reflection

1. What did you learn about communication in your family growing up? What part of those lessons have you brought into your marriage?
2. As you look at the list of what prevents good communication, what are you prone to do and why?
3. Review the different types of defenses you use and check which ones you go to when you are being triggered or feeling hurt. The more secure you become, the less defensive your responses, but you need to recognize them first.

For group discussion

1. Read the Connecting Conversation in the appendix. Where do your conversations usually break down? Applying the suggestions in the chapter on communication, try having a conversation with your partner or someone close. It takes practice to learn this skill. Active listening is like learning to ride a bike; it takes time and messing up occasionally until you are better at it.
2. Review the Four Quadrants of Relational Nutrients. Which skills do you need to develop? Think about your conversations. Do you start in quadrant 1 (the most effective place to start), or do you tend to start in quadrant 3 or 4? How about your spouse?
3. The Bible has much to say about communication. Read the following verses and write out what they say that applies to your prayer and thought life.

Surely you desire integrity in the inner self, and you teach me wisdom deep within. (Psalm 51:6 CSB)

Search me, God, and know my heart; test me and know my concerns. See if there is any offensive way in me; lead me in the everlasting way. (Psalm 139:23–24 CSB)

Not many should become teachers, my brothers, because you know that we will receive a stricter judgment. For we all stumble in many ways. If anyone does not stumble in what he says, he is mature, able also to control the whole body. Now if we put bits into the mouths of horses so that they obey us, we direct their whole bodies. And consider ships: Though very large and driven by fierce winds, they are guided by a very small rudder wherever the will of the pilot directs. So too, though the tongue is a small part of the body, it boasts great things. Consider how a small fire sets ablaze a large forest. And the tongue is a fire. The tongue, a world of unrighteousness, is placed among our members. It stains the whole body, sets the course of life on fire, and is itself set on fire by hell. Every kind of animal, bird, reptile, and fish is tamed and has been tamed by humankind, but no one can tame the tongue. It is a restless evil, full of deadly poison. With the tongue we bless our Lord and Father, and with it we curse people who are made in God's likeness. Blessing and cursing come out of the same mouth. My brothers and sisters, these things should not be this way. Does a spring pour out sweet and bitter water from the same opening? Can a fig tree produce olives, my brothers and sisters, or a grapevine produce figs? Neither can a saltwater spring yield fresh water. Who among you is wise and understanding? By his good conduct he should show that his works are done in the gentleness that comes from wisdom. But if you have bitter envy and selfish ambition in your heart, don't boast and deny the truth. Such wisdom does not come down from above but is earthly, unspiritual, demonic. For where there is envy and selfish ambition, there is disorder and every evil practice. But the wisdom from above is first pure, then peace-loving, gentle, compliant, full of mercy and good fruits, unwavering, without pretense. And the fruit of righteousness is sown in peace by those who cultivate peace. (James 3:1–18 CSB)

CHAPTER 9

Cycles of Change

When the whole world is running toward a cliff, he who is running
in the opposite direction appears to have lost his mind. The
right direction leads not only to peace but also to knowledge.

—Unknown

In the face of stressful situations in marriage, we frequently react
impulsively in our attempts to relieve our discomfort as soon as
possible. We don't pause, think, and pray before we act; we just act.
Knee-jerk reactions don't work well, but we just don't know what else
to do.

In the midst of stress, it's hard to know *how* to be in tune with
God's will and timing to make wise decisions or be aware *there is*
another way. We just want to feel better *now!* Rob and I tried to
change, but it never lasted. We'd be okay for a while, give up, then
try again six months later. It became a never-ending cycle of trying
to change, trying to do things differently but never truly changing.

Understanding cycles of change

Like a lot of men, Rob was good at asking, "What do I need to
do?" He was a task-oriented guy, and he believed his desire to change,
to learn, and to grow was enough to carry him to the next level. I was

guilty of thinking I would change as soon as Rob was different, making me totally dependent on his choices, giving him way too much power. The process of change is much more than having good desires and techniques. To experience a better path forward required that we both look at the cycles of change we were relying on. Our best thinking had gotten us where we were at the time, and we realized we needed to make a shift away from our perspectives about change.

You may identify with one of the cycles of change described below. My guess is, if you are asking, "What do I need to do?" you will find yourself in one of the first two cycles.

The Adjustment Cycle

Denial

Stability

Coping
Strategies

Refinement

Evaluation

- Learn to "cope"
- Learn to "change behaviors"
- Learn to "adjust"

The *Adjustment Cycle* is what we naturally do when dealing with change or upsetting events. In this stage, we use different strategies to cope with distress in our lives and make adjustments along the way. Then we evaluate and refine those strategies to see how they are working to achieve a greater sense of stability. In many ways, this cycle contributed to Rob's avoider tendencies and my vacillator tendencies. Although these strategies were useful for survival at times in our families, especially when we were young, most of the time, they were a Band-Aid approach that didn't deal with the real issues. The goal of the Adjustment Cycle is to find any means to avoid feeling bad.

The Therapeutic Cycle

Openness

Alignment

Insight

Support

Direction

- Want to "feel better"
- Want to "not hurt"
- Want "relief from pain"

The *Therapeutic Cycle* is an approach to gain insight and support, often with a counselor. As they offer insight and direction, we find alignment with the hope of finding relief. Again, this can be helpful short-term, but to simply "feel better" is not enough, and it is not the end goal. Not that this cycle is wrong, it's just not enough by itself. We stayed stuck in this cycle for years and wondered why we often walked out of a counselor's office and argued in the car all the way home. Without greater understanding of what's at the root of our issues, we didn't *feel* better. The pain persisted; it was just pushed down again.

The Spiritual Cycle

- **Freedom and Release**
- **Letting Go**
- **Compassion**

The *Spiritual Cycle* is a completely different approach to change. In this cycle, we start with an attitude of *brokenness*. I wonder if we resist this word because we assume brokenness means shattered to pieces. I have certainly felt that way, but *healthy* brokenness is really an admission of my fallibility, humanness, weakness, and poor coping skills. It's realizing our need for something outside of ourselves to solve life's problems but also to solve a problem we *can't* solve on our own. We need a savior, not just for eternal life but also for the here and now because our natural efforts always fall short.

From healthy *brokenness*, the spiritual cycle leads to *repentance* and turning from our old ways and habits. Next, we *abandon* or let go of the things we cling to for relief. This leads to increased *confidence* in God when we see He can be trusted to empower and guide us, eventually leading to *release* and freedom. Most of the time, when I was in distress, my longing and crying out to God came from not wanting to hurt any longer; I wanted relief. What I really needed was *release* from the ties I didn't even know were keeping me stuck, like fear of abandonment.

When I've asked couples over the years what surrender looks like to them, they often say *giving up* or *defeat*, which is familiar programming in our society. Something inside us rejects the thought of giving up. It's a powerless feeling. But what if there's wisdom in surrender, and it's not a sign of defeat?

Recently, I witnessed the rescue of a dolphin caught in a tangle of fishing line and weights. If not assisted, this beautiful creature would likely have died. Fighting to the point of exhaustion, this struggling dolphin was only thinking of escape and relief and was doing his best to break free, but the struggle was making the situation worse. He did not have the resources to free himself. When he finally surrendered to a team of caring people and allowed them to help, they were able to slowly cut the lines, and he was released to swim freely once again in the blue water without the encumbrance of the lines and weights.

Surrender and giving up are two different concepts. Giving up says, "What's the use?" Surrender says, "There is hope in a better way." Giving up says, "I can't." Surrender says, "I can't, but God can." Giving up is often expressed in anger. Surrender is expressed in love and humility. In God's economy, surrender is an acknowledgment of who really has the power to set things right. Surrender is *giving in*, rather than *giving up*.

We stayed in the first two cycles for over twenty years, looking for a *fix* to our situation. But as we've said before, people are not machines to be fixed but living, breathing creatures to be explored and understood. As I became secure enough to look at my own brokenness, my trust in God's love and care for me grew. He became to me the caring, comforting, and nurturing Father, who is the real source of change. This was difficult because I often viewed God like my earthly father, who was often not tender, caring, understanding, or supportive. This is where the body of Christ comes in. In an authentic community that reflected God's love, I found acceptance and encouragement to make hard choices and changes. My view and confidence in God also grew and went deeper.

The first step in any recovery program is admitting I am powerless (over alcohol, anger, pornography, reactivity, etc.) and my life is unmanageable. It begins with an admission of brokenness. In your case, you might not feel you're that bad; you might think admitting your life is unmanageable is reserved for really messed-up people, and you don't struggle in that way. But Scripture affirms no matter how cleaned up we look on the outside, we are broken from birth and need a savior, not just for our sin but to be released and freed to live life in a meaningful way today.

In their book *Love Focused*,[28] Bob and Judy Hughes offer their perspective on the differences among these cycles.

> Traditional psychology has taught us that our present behavior is the combined results of our childhood upbringing and our past experiences… Our past experiences certainly do have a large influence on how we act today. Things like childhood traumas, family dynamics, divorce, parental addictions, abuse, and many other experiences understandably affect people in many negative ways. However, while our past certainly does influence our present behavior, it does not make us behave in any particular way today… Thinking this way locks us into a victim mentality and reduces our responsibility for how we respond today.

Hughes is making the point that we still have choices. Therapy can be necessary and helpful, and God often uses it, but it is not the only way. Although we went to many counselors, we had work to do outside the counseling office, and we gave God room to work in our hearts in many different ways and through many different experiences. As we surrendered to God and took responsibility for our choices, we found healing through many different sources. It doesn't always require years of counseling to heal childhood wounds before seeing positive changes, but it starts with a choice to not stay locked up as a victim to our past.

---

[28] Bob Hughes and Judy Hughes, *Love Focused* (Crossroads Publishing, 2008).

The importance of being in community

Up to this point, we've offered information that helped us change on our journey. We hope this helps you see yourself, your spouse, and your relationship with God in a new light. But please be aware, we've only scratched the surface. We know you are going through challenges you were not made to handle alone. We were designed to live with others in a community, and although it can be messy at times, finding the right people to share your journey is indispensable but often overlooked.

One of the biggest mistakes we see in the lives of couples in the midst of pain is they isolate themselves from others. Staying connected with others who will support, listen, and encourage while offering balanced feedback and input from a biblical perspective is vital to your individual spiritual health as well as your connection as a couple. If this describes you, you are not unusual, and you are not alone. It requires men taking the initiative to pursue connection with other men who live from their values and integrity and women connecting with other mature women who can offer perspective and support. As a couple you will also benefit greatly from relationships with other supportive, growing, and understanding couples.

What to avoid

What we *don't do* is sometimes just as important as what we *do*. We offer some suggestions and cautions for what to avoid:

Avoid being overly confident

Being confident that Christ *can* heal your relationship is good, but if you're not careful, you can become overly confident God will do this just because you've asked. The danger in being overly confident that you can change your relationship on your own is assuming you have more power than you have. This borders on ignorance or pride. Healing involves not just God's will but also the choices of someone else, who may or may not yet be willing.

As hard as it is, be patient as God works in both of you to learn what needs to be learned. While it might have some theological flaws, someone shared this definition of submission that got my attention: "Roxanne, you may need to bow low enough in humility before God and let Him work on you so Rob has to face himself." When our controlling behavior gets in the way, it becomes easier for our partners to shift the responsibility for change away from themselves and back onto the other person.

Avoid making hasty decisions

If you are in a situation in your marriage where you feel backed into a corner or forced to make a quick decision and feel confused, God's counsel in his word is to wait:

> The greedy stir up conflict, but those who
> trust in the Lord will prosper.
> Those who trust in themselves are fools,
> but those who walk in wisdom are kept safe.
> (Proverbs 28:25–26 NIV)

We watched many couples make quick, irrational decisions because they felt pressured by others and were tired of feeling confused. God does not work that way. Waiting on God and knowing He will guide you is a hard concept for many to grasp, but that's exactly what He wants to do. God wants to guide you through His Word, other believers, and the Holy Spirit, but it's hard to hear these voices when you're running scared.

Avoid too many counselors

The book of Proverbs tells us there is wisdom in the counsel of others. When having relationship problems, it's dangerous to get opinions from too many people. If this describes you, you've probably also experienced the problems that come when too many people get involved; everyone has a different answer to your problem. We've found it's best to keep your "advice circle" to about three or four people you respect, people who are not biased, are honest, and whose interpretation and use of biblical wisdom resonates with your faith commitments. Parents and close friends tend to give advice to make you happy, and when they know too many details about your marriage problems, it can create negative feelings toward your partner.

Another reason to avoid too many counselors is that it can take away dependence on God to meet your deepest needs through being still and listening in prayer. This is based on learning how to hear from God directly and developing greater sensitivity to how he may be leading you. Sometimes when I've asked God for wisdom or perspective, I get a clear impression or a thought or a repeated message from many sources, like a sermon or a verse in the Bible or even the same message from a book. It's about making myself more open to listening.

Making decisions primarily based on advice from others without the important step of personal communication with God is incomplete. As wise and well-intended as the wisdom from your friends and counselor might be, they are still human. You need wisdom from above.

Avoid rescuing and "playing God"

Many well-meaning Christians have difficulty letting people suffer the consequences of sin or foolishness, especially when it comes to our spouse or children. This is an important principle to learn because if you continue getting in the way of God's lessons for those you love (or allow others to get in the way of your lessons), it takes much longer to grow and becomes more painful in the end.

If your spouse behaves in a way that causes painful consequences in his or her life—such as in the workplace, with the law, or with friends—your role is to love, encourage, and pray for him or her, but be cautious about taking on the responsibility of fixing the situation. It usually results in resentment because it feels parental. Your adult spouse doesn't need another parent. When we rescue our loved ones, they are less likely to learn what they need to learn, and you risk losing a measure of respect for them. The unconscious result of rescuing partners from their problems increases the risk of seeing themselves as unable to get out of their own *mess* without your help.

Avoid being paralyzed by fear

The opposite of faith is not doubt or unbelief. The opposite of faith is fear. Many couples never reconcile simply because they fear being hurt, embarrassed, or disappointed again. That was my issue. But as I learned to face my fear, I chose to believe my soul was secure because of Christ and His love and care for me. Putting my confidence in God, I knew I would survive even if Rob did something hurtful. As a result, I was able to courageously speak up. I learned how to appropriately say no, ask for help, and communicate what was okay and what was not. There were also times God invited me to be silent, wait, and trust Him.

When God's Word contradicts your feelings, especially fear, acknowledge the feelings and explore what they are tied to, but let your Father in heaven lead you. Your feelings matter, and God wants you to pour out your heart to Him, but making decisions based on fear rather than God's leading is a sure sign you're not following His voice.

> When God reveals a truth, the paralysis of
> refusing to act leaves a man exactly where he was
> before. But once he acts, he is never the same.[29]

Avoid comparing your marriage with others

This is an obvious statement but more difficult to avoid than we realize. From the outside looking in, everyone's marriage looked

---

[29] Oswald Chambers, *My Utmost for His Highest*, Ed. James Reimann (Oswald Chambers Publications Assn., Ltd., 1992).

better than ours. But behind closed doors, the picture often looks vastly different. Even songs and movies made me feel sorry for myself as I made this comparison mistake. All God's people have challenges, some more than others, but comparing only leads to envy or pride, and neither are good options.

Comparing your marriage to someone else's causes pain and frustration. You won't be able to live up to the expectations you put on your spouse and yourself. God purposely and intentionally created each of you, and as a result, your marriage has its own personality and struggles based on your unique history and temperaments.

Comparison is the thief of joy and the stretcher of truth. Comparison says, "What's wrong with us?" Or it can accuse you of being ill-equipped for the journey of growth and change. The truth is, God has given you what you need for what He has set before you. The truth of His Word says that He prepared us for good works, and every good thing comes from Him.

Comparison comes from a distorted focus. Putting your eyes on the things in front of others rather than what is in front of you leads to being discontented with what you have. Comparing yourself to others causes you to lose focus and minimize your own abundance.

Avoid outcome-focused goals

Without realizing it, I lived with so many expectations of what I believed should or needed to happen in my marriage, in my relationship with God—you name it. The tricky part was, to me, they seemed right and reasonable. I camped on the "Love Languages" and felt justified that Rob *needed* to meet those desires for me to be whole or happy. Because we live in a broken world where pain and disappointment are a reality, in our flesh, we organize our lives around avoiding pain. This causes us to come up with our own goals and expected outcomes, especially when we don't really believe God will provide what we need. This becomes our primary goal instead of loving well.

In their book *Love Focused*, Bob and Judy Hughes coined the term "Outcome-Focused Goals," and this approach unknowingly keeps us from being free to love well and to handle stress and disappointments in healthy ways. These are a few *outcome-focused goals* we struggled with:

- I need others to love me (to get the respect I think I deserve).
- I need my spouse to meet my needs (because I'm not sure God is enough).
- I need my spouse to understand me and see things my way (to feel good about myself).
- I need to keep my spouse or children happy with me (so they will think I'm a good person).
- I need to get my children to turn out okay (so others will think I'm a good parent).
- I need others to see me as competent (to prove I'm enough).

Needs versus desires

There's nothing wrong with having desires or wants. I want a good, supportive, affectionate relationship. I want to live in a nice home. I want my kids to be successful. But when my desire is elevated to a need, it becomes a demand or a "have to" that sets me up for anger, stress, and frustration. Then depression sets in when I've lost hope my *outcome-focused goals* will be achieved.

When a *desire* is not met, it's appropriate to be sad or disappointed. But as soon as I say I *need* something, it can become compulsive. What I *need* borders on idolatry and begins to control me. By definition, a compulsion is *self-centered*, and I become *self-focused* as I become fixated on getting my way. These compulsions don't always have to be alcohol, drugs, or food; they can also be relational demands.

For example, due to my insecurities, I believed I needed Rob's constant assurance that I was beautiful, wanted, and valued, which he wasn't great at offering. I also wanted to avoid the pain of rejection or feeling "less than." So I would ask, plead, argue, and sometimes demand this need, when in reality, I needed to find my security and value in how God sees me and receive Rob's encouragement as a welcome addition.

No one can fill in the hole of fears and insecurities from childhood; only God gives the meaning and value we seek. The bottom line, we will either minister to one another or manipulate, and we can only minister if we are assured we are fully loved and accepted by God.

Love-focused goals

In contrast to *outcome-focused goals*, *love-focused goals* are those that reflect my choices and attitude, which are all I really have control over, such as:

- To love others well.
- To be a good mom.
- To explain myself with patience.
- To speak the truth in love.
- To enforce the rules with my son.
- To focus on the good.
- To grow in my trust of God's

A *love-focused* approach is more about my attitude, my choices, and trusting God rather than strategies to make sure my emotional needs are met or avoiding and eliminating pain.

> Clearly, if we lived like God loved us, we'd be more able to trust him to meet our needs. As a result, we'd be freer to let go of our own agenda and follow God's plan.[30]

---

[30] Hughes.

God is enough

The shift in thinking for me was believing and trusting God was for me, fully offering and wanting to uphold me, share my pain and empower me even when the humans around me weren't as loving as I would like. When I fix my gaze on people and the world *first* to meet my needs, rather than trusting God, my spouse becomes a threat to my security.

God is more than enough, and He is there for me as I learn how to love my spouse and myself better. Even though He's often a mystery to me and I've bitterly complained when I think *I* know best what should happen and when, I've seen over and over again, His way is better than mine. Placing my trust in the only source of full knowledge and wisdom rather than my limited understanding is not blind trust; it's an act of surrender. When my intentional practice is to surrender to God and listen for His guidance, I am more at peace with myself and those around me even when there are disappointments.

God has certainly used people to bring me comfort, direction, and encouragement, for which I'm so grateful, but knowing God is the true source of hope, peace, and comfort enables me to constantly say, "Regardless of what happens, my soul is secure."

Discussion Questions

Chapter 9: Cycles of Change

For personal reflection

1. Which cycle of change have you used the most and why?
2. Are you merely looking for pain relief, or do you want release from things that are keeping you stuck? Why?
3. The spiritual cycle starts with brokenness (admitting we don't have all the answers or power). What areas of brokenness are you becoming aware of? Write about this.
4. To what extent is *fear* a factor for you? What is the earliest age you recall feeling fearful? When did fear begin when you were young? Fear is common to all of us, but some of us struggle with it more, or we just get better at covering it up. Make a list of your fears and ask God to give His perspective and grace in dealing with them. Ninety-five percent of the things I feared never happened, but I lost sleep for years over them.
5. What are some of your *outcome-focused goals*? Make a list of your desires and ask yourself if you think you *need* them to be whole, or are you asking a person to provide what God wants to give you?

For group discussion

1. There are many things to avoid in the process of change. As you read about what to avoid, which ones do you need to pay attention to and why? Write out one small decision you can make in that area to help keep you on the path of growth. For example, if you tend to make hasty decisions, one small step would be to wait twenty-four hours or even thirty days, depending on the decision, before deciding. Use this time to calm any strong emotions or reactivity so

you can hear God and think more clearly before deciding anything.

2. Read the verse below and write about what you can count on during challenging times.

Do not fear, for I am with you;
do not be afraid, for I am your God.
I will strengthen you; I will help you;
I will hold on to you with my righteous right hand. (Isaiah 41:10)

CHAPTER 10

Where Do We Go from Here?

> ALICE: "Would you tell me, please, which way I ought to go from here?"
>
> THE CHESHIRE CAT: "That depends a good deal on where you want to get to."
>
> ALICE: "I don't much care where."
>
> THE CHESHIRE CAT: "Then it doesn't much matter which way you go."
>
> ALICE: "Just as long as I get somewhere."
>
> THE CHESHIRE CAT: "Oh, you're sure to do that, if only you walk long enough." [39]
>
> —Lewis Carroll, *Alice's Adventures in Wonderland*

"You're sure to get somewhere...if you walk long enough." Anyone familiar with the story of Alice in Wonderland has read the encounter between Alice and the Cheshire Cat. The cat gives a witty-yet-sarcastic reply but with a painful element of truth. If you don't know where you want to go, it really doesn't matter which way you walk.

As we entered our journey of restoration, we realized we didn't have a very good picture of what a healthy relationship looks like, where we were going, and had no clue how to get there. We are grateful for others along the way who encouraged, supported, and guided us. As you have patiently read some of our story, we hope you recognized a few landmarks and road signs of what it looks like to be moving in a healthy direction. We've made progress but certainly know we haven't arrived. Patience and acceptance of our uniqueness, our similarities, and our differences go a long way.

Lessons from the climb

Some years ago, we visited Italy with another couple. It was our first trip to Italy, we didn't speak the language, and GPS or cell phone navigation was not sophisticated enough to guide us throughout Italy. Our first stay was in the small town of Vernazza in a beautiful coastal area called Cinque Terre. This region is known for colorful towns built into hillsides connected by hiking trails among the villages. We booked our B and B accommodations through the help of the well-known Rick Steves tour book, and the vague directions and instructions from our B and B host were to "look for a green gate along the path." Rick Steves's guidebook mentioned in the fine print, "It might be a bit of a climb" to get to our lodging, but I took that to mean *feet*, not *miles*.

With bags in tow, we started climbing the dirt trail leading out of Vernazza. I was hopeful. After all, it was just a single path; we had directions and instructions to look for a green gate, so how hard could it be? By this time, it was 10:00 p.m., and there were no lights, just a full moon to guide us. I hiked ahead because Rob and our friends were carrying heavier bags, so I thought I would scout out the location and then call down to them. As I kept climbing, I passed green gate after green gate. In fact, every house we passed had a green gate, and it seemed like everyone in Italy painted their gate green. Now all I had was a house number, and most of the house numbers were missing or hidden by overgrown vines.

Climbing the steep path, I quietly cursed Rick Steves under my breath for minimizing this part of the journey just to sell an exciting adventure in his guidebook. I was sure we were lost on the side of a mountain in a foreign country late at night, and I honestly believed we would be sleeping *alfresco*. The four of us were spread out over this dark trail and at times couldn't see each other, but I didn't panic, although I started to feel all alone. I looked up at the moon and prayed, "God, have mercy on us. We are lost. I don't have a clue where we should go. Please guide our steps."

Still climbing, I became more and more certain we'd been led astray. I was almost at the point of giving up, but as I turned the next corner, the light of the moon illuminated a stone arch with a faded green gate and the right house number. After passing through the stone arch, I looked up and saw the house was still another hundred steps up.

The next morning, I was sure there must have been an easier way to get to this place, so as the sun was rising, I made my way outside for a panorama view of our surroundings. From our hillside perch, I could see the mountains, the cliffs, the sea below, but there was no other road. The rugged footpath we had taken was the only way up or down. We were shocked we ever found the house in the dark.

Not to compare the two, but because of the difficult climb and the heavy bags we carried, we nicknamed this trail "Via Dolorosa" (Christ's road of pain to the cross). We stayed at this B and B for four days, and each day, we hiked down to the village (often complaining all the way). That was until one Sunday morning when we were passed by locals traveling the trail to get to the next town. An older woman, looking to be in her eighties, was navigating the trail just fine as she briskly walked past us and offered a cheerful *Buon Giorno*. We were humbled. We had an expectation the road should be easier, and this sweet old woman had likely traveled this path on a regular basis and was no doubt healthier for it. She knew the path and had adjusted her expectations.

> Growth of any kind is a hard path, and any
> expectation that it should be easy is an illusion.

That was the first of many weird twists and turns we experienced on our *unguided* tour of Italy. This trip was years ago, and all we had at the time were paper maps. I often found myself praying for His grace and direction as I leaned on Him in a dependent way. The wonderful part of this trip was how I experienced God and His grace in a more tangible way than I have in other travels, even when we finally had more advanced navigation technology.

When God is all you have, you have all you need. When we rely on ourselves alone or other forms of security to get by, God is no less caring of us, but we may not experience the fullness of His love, tenderness, and care. I usually want the easy road, maybe from fear of failure, but on this trip, I learned He's always with me, even if the road is challenging or hard. In the end, that's the best place to be.

The way forward

In the midst of pain and crisis, the path forward looks dark and impossible. When I was in that place, it felt like there was no way out. Like throwing mud on the wall, we tried one thing after another, hoping the next counselor would offer something that would stick and make a difference. Along our dark path, God gave us people, books, and new understanding that helped. As we've explored and unpacked what we learned along the way, we've offered some of the bread crumbs that guided our steps. We rarely had crystal clear guidance or turn-by-turn directions. These skills and new habits of the heart helped our marriage and made a difference, *not* because they are magic but because we trusted God to empower us to change as we applied them. So it was a mixture of being open and teachable and persistent enough to apply what we'd learned even when the road was rough.

The chapters in this book have been organized to provide a road map to a healthier and more secure marriage. Yes, it is our experience, but in working with so many couples through their journey of pain, broken trust, and loss of hope, we have seen and believe that repair and restoration are possible. One of our first steps was honestly looking at our early years without minimizing or denying. This required a willingness to see and *own* the ways our histories were impacting our present relationships. We were then able to recognize our need for change as we adjusted our false *thinking* and *beliefs*, the origins of so much of our reactivity.

Along the way, we began to see how our *self-images* were wrapped up with the opinions of others, our acceptance was performance-based, and we believed love was *earned*. At different times, we worked through *trust issues* while we learned how to be safe and trustworthy with each other. This moved us in the direction of tackling our *broken intimacy*, understanding our *love styles*, and how to interrupt our *unhealthy patterns*. Lastly, we continue to work on *communicating* in healthy and understanding ways.

As mentioned in several chapters, when we aren't in touch with the source of our reactivity, it is difficult to apply helpful tools. So even though most couples say their immediate need is better communication, God often has a different agenda, and a foundation of awareness and compassion needs to be built in order to hear and see each other in a meaningful way.

Looking for help

Because so many of us didn't learn healthy skills of relating growing up, we may need the assistance of the right counselor or coach. I say "right counselor" because we found many counselors who sympathized and cared but didn't provide clear direction or practical steps. Others didn't challenge our unhealthy thoughts and beliefs or call us to anything higher than our own relief or comfort, even suggesting divorce at times.

Some counselors were *Christians*, but they didn't help us explore the spiritual part of our lives or how our spiritual values influenced our relational patterns. If we truly are made up of three parts—mind, body, and soul—then all three are important in healing the whole person. As a vacillator, I needed help seeing my blind spots without defensiveness and shame. My responsibility was to be the best version of myself, no matter what Rob did, and not measure our problems on a scale to see who was more at fault. Waiting for Rob to be more spiritual and loving before I would was faulty thinking I needed to change. As an avoider, Rob worked on becoming secure enough to open up, share feelings, be more courageous, face conflict, and change his unhealthy ways of coping.

For a couple to experience true repair, both partners need to be responsible for their individual work of growth and healing. You may feel progress is slow at times, and it was for us as well. But I was determined to embrace the process of growth and change even if Rob wasn't ready yet.

We are so thankful to Larry Crabb, who gave us a vision of what godly relating looks like while at the same time showing us lovingly (and sometimes bluntly) where we both fell short. As you look for wisdom, look for advisers with a combination of grace and truth, who truly live in close communion with God and offer guidance not based solely on education or credentials but by how they listen to God on your behalf. This might be a challenge, but at least if you know what you're looking for, you won't be groping up a hillside in the dark looking for a green gate.

You are not alone

There isn't one right way to resolve relational breakdowns, and our story will not be exactly like yours, but we hope our experience helps you see you are not alone. We pray that our journey through the troubled waters of marriage will give you hope and a bit of coaching on how to navigate your own white water rapids. We have met so many couples just like us over the years and have become convinced we are more alike than different in our relational struggles. Be aware that your unhealthy patterns of relating are only symptoms showing where you need to grow, not only with each other but also in your relationship with God.

You've heard the old Chinese proverb, "A journey of a thousand miles begins with a single step." We started one step at a time, and we hope you will too. Believe it or not, real growth doesn't happen in leaps and bounds but in small consistent steps in the right direction. You can rest in knowing God is for you, and He wants your growth even more than you do. He is more powerful, loving (and yes, at times confusing) than we will ever know, so we walk by faith, not by sight, with the full assurance of knowing He wastes nothing. God used our pain, our brokenness, and our darkness, as well as joy, release, and freedom in ways we could never have imagined.

After all, isn't that why we're here: to be free to love God and love others in our pain, through our pain, to eventually bring a tiny bit of heaven to this broken world until we get to experience total wholeness one day in eternity.

Leaving a legacy

You influence people every day by what you say and do, and all of that influence adds up. But your legacy is not just about you and what you've created; it's about the story God is writing. What does leaving a legacy mean to you? Maybe it means leaving a mark in a way that makes a difference to future generations. Whatever you are doing, you are building something you will leave behind, something that will outlive you.

Your story is never just about you. We are all part of a larger narrative. Events, actions, and people intersect with our stories, and our challenge is to see the bigger picture beyond our own story to recognize how these stories have shaped us and how we impact others.

The stakes are high when we think of the legacy we leave behind. As we look at our family picture below, we think of how different it would have been if we hadn't made hard decisions to humble ourselves, be willing to change, take risks, act courageously, and learn new habits of the heart to love well. We encourage you to pull out a family picture, put it somewhere you will see every day, and consider what's at stake for you. Find a big-enough reason to take bold and courageous steps.

We found twenty-one reasons to build a legacy that lasts in the faces below. What's yours?

Discussion Questions

Chapter 10: Where Do We Go from Here?

For personal reflection

1. Write out when you felt lost or confused and it was hard to hear from God. Then write about when you felt more trusting of God and you had a sense of peace. Compare the two and look for what you were doing differently during peaceful times.
2. What have you read in this book that provided perspective, hope, or peace? Is there an invitation from God you need to follow or apply?
3. If you are reading this book alone, consider joining a group for support. Groups create a powerful learning experience, and there is much to learn from each other as we share our joy, our pain, and our questions along the way.

For group discussion

1. What is the real foundation for your hope? Is it only in your spouse changing, a child behaving, or any other person becoming different?
2. What legacy are you leaving? It may not be a perfect picture, but what will you do today to influence the lives around you in a positive way?
3. Review the suggested reading list. We included a selection of books that had a profound influence on our growth and healing. Talk with your group on the next steps you are going to take.
4. Check out our website *iSightCoaching.com*, where you can view videos and other resources on topics discussed in this book.

CALM ME INTO A QUIETNESS

Now,
O Lord,
calm me into a quietness
that heals
and listens,
and molds my longings
and passions,
my wounds
and wonderings
into a more holy
and human
shape.

—Ted Loder, *Guerillas of Grace*[31]

---

[31] Ted Loder, *Guerrillas of Grace: Prayers for the Battle* (Augsburg Books, 2005).

APPENDIX

Recommended books

- *How We Love*, Milan and Kay Yerkovich (attachment recovery)
- *Love Focused*, Bob and Judy Hughes
- *Boundaries for the Soul*, Allison Cook and Kimberly Miller
- *Torn Asunder*, Dave Carder (affair recovery)
- *Shattered Dreams*, Larry Crabb
- *Understanding Who You Are*, Larry Crabb
- *Seven Principles for Making Marriage Work*, John M. Gottman
- *The Silence of Adam*, Larry Crabb
- *Sacred Marriage*, Gary Thomas
- *When the Soul Listens*, Jan Johnson
- *Unwanted*, Jay Stringer
- *What Happened to You?* Dr. Bruce Perry and Oprah Winfrey

Recommended weekly connecting questions

Any of the *Soul* or *Relational* questions are a good start for a connecting conversation.

Soul questions

1. Give me two to three feeling words to describe where you are now. What do you think these feelings are tied to?

2. Is there anything you are particularly anxious about this week or anything you are particularly at peace about?
3. Is there anything that happened this week that triggered an emotional response in you, and what did you do about it?
4. Are there specific pressures or emotions you are feeling now?

Relational questions

1. How have you experienced me this week? What's it been like to live with me? (a brave question).
2. Is there anything that happened between us this week that you felt led to confusion, misunderstanding, or miscommunication?
3. On a one-to-ten scale, how close have you felt to me this week?
4. What have I done this week that you appreciated?
5. What would help you not retreat into an old pattern this week, such as avoiding, distracting, pushing others away, being overly pleasing, etc.?
6. Is there some way I could or did comfort you?
7. How can I help you in your specific role and responsibilities this week?

Spirit questions

1. Where have you experienced God's encouragement or empowerment this week?
2. How can I pray for you this week?

FEELINGS LIST (SOUL WORDS)

Developing and increasing your *emotional vocabulary* is *important* because it helps you have more answers than "Good," "Fine," "Okay," or "Not so good" when someone asks about how you're doing. Giving a value (such as *good* or *bad*) to your *feelings* can reinforce shame and guilt, which handicaps your ability to identify and recognize your *feelings*. The earlier you develop an emotional vocabulary—and it's never too early or too late to start—the better your chances of cultivating emotional maturity, inner growth, and improving your communication and connection.

- *Happy*: cheerful, delighted, elated, encouraged, glad, gratified, joyful, lighthearted, overjoyed, pleased, relieved, satisfied, thrilled, secure.
- *Loving*: affectionate, cozy, passionate, romantic, sexy, warm, tender, responsive, thankful, appreciative, refreshed, pleased.
- *High energy*: energetic, enthusiastic, excited, playful, rejuvenated, talkative, pumped, motivated, driven, determined, obsessed.
- *Amazed*: stunned, surprised, shocked, jolted.
- *Anxious*: uneasy, embarrassed, frustrated, nauseated, ashamed, nervous, restless, worried, stressed.
- *Confident*: positive, secure, self-assured, assertive.
- *Peaceful*: at ease, calm, comforted, cool, relaxed, serene.
- *Afraid*: scared, anxious, apprehensive, boxed in, burdened, confused, distressed, fearful, frightened, guarded, hard-

pressed, overwhelmed, panicky, paralyzed, tense, terrified, worried, insecure.

- *Traumatized*: shocked, disturbed, injured, damaged.
- *Angry*: annoyed, controlled, manipulated, furious, grouchy, grumpy, irritated, provoked, frustrated.
- *Low energy*: beaten down, exhausted, tired, weak, listless, depressed, detached, withdrawn, indifferent, apathetic.
- *Alone*: avoidant, lonely, abandoned, deserted, forlorn, isolated, cutoff, detached.
- *Sad*: unhappy, crushed, dejected, depressed, desperate, despondent, grieved, heartbroken, heavy, weepy.
- *Betrayed*: deceived, fooled, duped, tricked.
- *Confused*: baffled, perplexed, mystified, bewildered.
- *Ashamed*: guilty, mortified, humiliated, embarrassed, exposed.

ATTACHMENT CORE PATTERN THERAPY®
VACILLATOR/AVOIDER CORE PATTERN
© 2013 Milan and Kay Resources, Inc.
www.howwelove.com

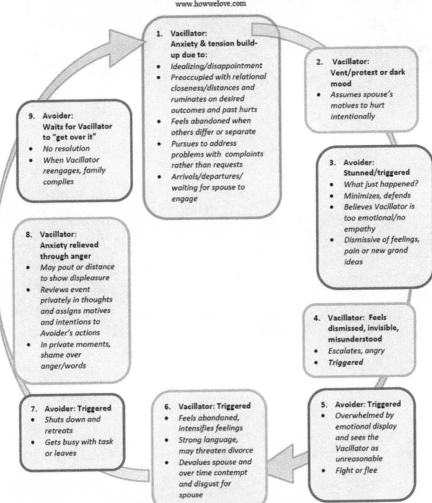

This is just one of the attachment core patterns. Other combinations can be found at *HowWeLove.com.*

THE PATH THROUGH CONFLICT

When conflict arises, we have a choice of two paths: the Path of Protection or the Path of Growth. The Path of Protection will look defensive and closed, while the Path of Growth will look nondefensive and open. One path is fueled by the intent to protect against pain and fear, while the other is fueled by the intent to learn. One path avoids personal responsibility, and the other accepts and owns behavior, feelings, and consequences.

In the end, the path to self-protect will lead to negative consequences, power struggles, distance, feeling unloved, and greater pain. The path to growth leads to intimacy, joy in the relationship, improved conflict resolution, and personal freedom. Review the following diagram and discuss what you see in yourself and in your relationship regarding these two paths. Where do you get stuck?

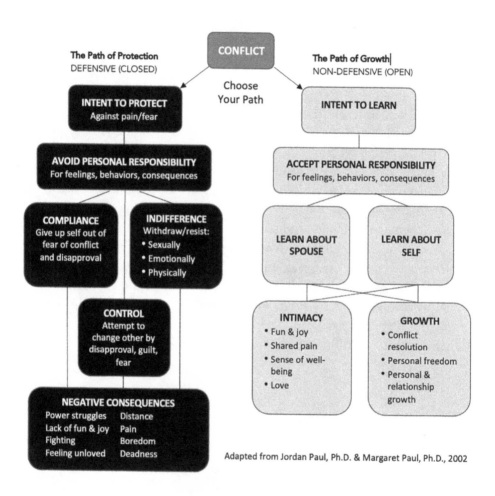

Adapted from Jordan Paul, Ph.D. & Margaret Paul, Ph.D., 2002

ABOUT THE AUTHOR

For the past fifteen years, Rob and Roxanne Maroney have been helping couples rebuild relationships threatened by lack of intimacy, lost connection, damaged love styles, and broken trust. As a trained counselor and life coach, Roxanne works with women and couples to help heal and repair broken relationships. Rob spent twenty-five years in the corporate world with major international companies and now works with a nonprofit counseling and teaching ministry. Rob works with men recovering from sexual integrity issues.

They both have educational backgrounds in psychology, biblical counseling, and Christian life coaching. They are certified in Gottman Therapist Training and are SYMBIS (Saving Your Marriage Before It Starts) facilitators.

Rob and Roxanne live in Orange County, California, and have been married for over four decades. They have three grown children and thirteen grandchildren. From their own experience of repair and recovery, Rob and Roxanne share openly and candidly what they learned about building a marriage to last. *Hope after Hurt* is a story that needs to be told to give hope to those in need.

CPSIA information can be obtained
at www.ICGtesting.com
Printed in the USA
JSHW021015201022
31826JS00004B/32